happy hens
& fresh eggs

·························

KEEPING CHICKENS
IN THE KITCHEN GARDEN

with 100 Recipes

happy hens & fresh eggs

KEEPING CHICKENS IN THE KITCHEN GARDEN

with 100 Recipes

SIGNE LANGFORD

WITH PHOTOGRAPHS
BY DONNA GRIFFITH

Douglas & McIntyre

CLOCKWISE FROM TOP: Noella, my blue-egg-laying rumpless Araucana (Signe Langford photo); a pot of arugula seedlings for the ladies (SL); Baby, my cuddly hen (Donna Griffith photo); pretty pale blue potato blossoms (SL). PREVIOUS SPREAD: Big Mamma in fall asters (SL).

Douglas and McIntyre (2013) Ltd.
P.O. Box 219, Madeira Park, BC, VON 2HO
www.douglas-mcintyre.com

EDITED BY Carol Pope and Nicola Goshulak
INDEXED BY Nicola Goshulak
COVER AND TEXT DESIGN BY Mauve Pagé
PHOTOS BY Donna Griffith unless otherwise noted
ILLUSTRATIONS BY Sophia Saunders
PRINTED AND BOUND IN Canada
PRINTED ON FSC-certified paper made with
10% post-consumer waste

Canadä

Canada Council   Conseil des arts
for the Arts   du Canada

BRITISH COLUMBIA
ARTS COUNCIL
An agency of the Province of British Columbia

Douglas and McIntyre (2013) Ltd. acknowledges the support of the Canada Council for the Arts, which last year invested $157 million to bring the arts to Canadians throughout the country. We also gratefully acknowledge financial support from the Government of Canada through the Canada Book Fund and from the Province of British Columbia through the BC Arts Council and the Book Publishing Tax Credit.

Cataloguing data available from Library and Archives Canada
ISBN 978-1-77162-097-0 (paper)
ISBN 978-1-77162-098-7 (ebook)

thank you!

It takes a village to write a book. And I'm blessed to be surrounded by a village of generous folks!

Massive thanks to volunteer recipe testers, my niece Wendy Roberts and her daughter Marlowe Coombes, Lynn Girard, Lisa Maria Diano (who also sewed my ladies some pretty new curtains to help protect their modesty when laying) and her daughter, Ginger, who thought the shirred eggs were so nice she made them twice!

Lynda Felton floofed the linens just so and dug deep into my cupboards and her own to find pretty things for a few of the recipe pictures. The talented and tolerant Donna Griffith took amazing photos in cramped spaces, with an annoying little dog threatening to eat the subject. Donna's assistants, Carmen Cheung and Lisa Daly, not only helped Donna, they modelled, went on emergency mid-recipe grocery runs, and tried to coax a natural smile out of yours truly for the author portrait. Not easy. Speaking of—a major shout out to makeup artist Alex Smith of Red Makeup who did a darned good job with this 50-year-old mug if I do say so myself!

The giving and talented Sophia Saunders created adorable hen sketches and whimsical garden illustrations, and freelance photographer and art director Colleen Nicholson inspired and instructed the now oft-viewed photo of me holding Miss Vicky in that crazy green and red coat.

I'm so grateful to all the celebrity chefs who shared recipes and stories even though they all have way bigger and better things to do than contribute to my little book. Such lovely true colours! And all the chicken bloggers, for sharing their wisdom and who are all more expert than I!

My nutty friend Elisabeth Burrow of Jewels Under the Kilt generously supplied me with her Ontario-grown pecans, and Murray's Farm in Cambridge, Ontario, lovingly offered up about a million pasture-raised eggs for all the recipe testing. My ladies simply could not squeeze 'em out fast enough!

The nice folks at Blue Diamond provided a case of Almond Breeze Chocolate Almond Milk to play with, and Rolling Meadows Dairy supplied me with the most wonderful grass-fed milk and butter from happy cows!

Crate & Barrel was lovely enough to send me some chicken linens, a pretty apron and sweet birdy egg cups to help make this book so pretty. Thanks also to the excellent folks at Ventures International for the Norpro gadgets I used in the kitchen; my new favourite thing: a set of measuring spoons that goes down to a "smidgeon."

Thanks to Trudeau Corporation for some helpful kitchenware, Danica for the lovely feather linens and gorgeous black rooster apron, and KitchenAid for my beloved, cherished, sexy black stand mixer. The delicate and pretty *coeur à la crème* moulds are from Art et Manufacture, and Blundstone—makers of those practically indestructible boots—supplied me with an awesome pair that I just adore for all my garden work. I mentioned red is kind of my thing; they heard me. Also, Swissmar sent me the coolest egg-capping gadget that neatly zapped the tops off of egg shells I used as serving vessels.

And last but *sooo* not least, my editor Carol Pope who is a saint/shrink/hand-holder/editing genius/calmer-downer of this freaking-out first-time book writer.

contents

preface

As a backyard gardener scratching away at growing edibles and building up my self-sufficiency, I've been asking *should I or shouldn't I* when it comes to keeping chickens. I'm hungry for delicious, ethical free-run eggs to feed my family, and keen for a fluffy flock that will patrol for garden pests and contribute bucket-loads of rich chicken manure for the vegetable beds.

But questions continue to cluck away inside my head: Are chickens worth the fuss? Will they rule the backyard roost, or are they easy company? Which breeds are best and what will they do to my gardens if I give them free reign? What can and can't they eat, and how about predators, parasites, winter freezes and summer heat spikes? And on and on I fuss, pretty much like (yes) an old hen.

Thankfully, in what is one of the most entertaining reads I've had in a good long while, author, chef and backyard-chicken fanatic Signe Langford answers all these questions and more, and tells how, with a tad of know-how, keeping chickens can be child's play. And, with all of their adorable antics to enjoy, just as fun.

Including tips for keeping a flock of happy egg-layers, what happens when a hen hits "henopause" and DIY chicken doctoring, Signe takes us through the year from a bird's-eye point of view and tells *all* about life at "Cluckingham Palace," her urban backyard henhouse. She offers advice on which plants to grow, and how to protect them from the "cutest walking garburators ever," as

Child's play: hen-keeping is fun and so worth the extra effort. Here Marlowe hams it up with Helen, a blind "ex-bat" who contentedly lived out her last days in the author's backyard henhouse.

well as a plan for the ultimate herb garden for healthy hens.

When eggs—gorgeous blue from Ameraucana chickens or rich chocolate-brown from Marans—are as good as only homegrown eggs can be, their flavour shines through. With spectacular photography by Donna Griffith, this book provides over a hundred seasonal ways, many contributed by top chefs, to enjoy the abundance and versatility of backyard eggs.

This beautiful collection of recipes, reminiscences and sage advice will inspire and delight with its many reflections on the joys and deep satisfaction of adding happy hens and fresh eggs to our everyday life.

—Carol Pope, Associate Editor

OPPOSITE, CLOCKWISE FROM TOP LEFT: Miss Vicky shrugging off the cold (DG); tomato and bleeding heart seedlings in eggshell pots (DG); Big Mamma, hanging out inside for a change (DG); peach blossoms in my spring garden (DG).

introduction

My father had a weakness for strays, so I grew up with an ever-changing menagerie that waxed and waned as they came and went. Some, too broken or dependent to go back to the wild, stayed; others were eager to heal and head for home. He had a soft spot for the rejected and unwanted, the maligned, the mangy, the motley and even the nefarious: raccoons, skunks, crows, a caiman he must have smuggled back with us from Florida, even a lonely squirrel monkey he spotted at the mall. And, of course, there were all the usual suspects: canaries, budgies, dogs, rabbits, hamsters, fish and a funky-smelling stray tomcat named Wally Walnuts, along with the ducks and chickens. It all seemed perfectly normal to me.

I loved all the animals, but it was the unique relationship we humans can have with chickens

BELOW: My garden, circa 2009 BC (that's Before Chickens). I ended up trading in my lush backyard meadow for fresh eggs and feathered friends.
OPPOSITE, CLOCKWISE FROM TOP LEFT: Miss Vicky and me (DG); red potato blossoms (SL); pumpkin tendril (SL); Cindy Loo, a rescued Silkie (SL).

SIGNE LANGFORD PHOTO

DONALD LANGFORD PHOTO

My affection for birds of all feathers goes way, way back. My childhood was richer for keeping hens, and I can't imagine life without my ladies now, either.

going out on a limb

The whole time I've had my ladies I've been on edge; I feel like we're living on borrowed time. You see, in my town, keeping a few lovely backyard hens goes against a municipal bylaw that was written into the books in 1987. The group Toronto Chickens, spearheaded by my good friend "Dar Len" (yes, that's her *nom de plume*—literally!) has been working tirelessly to have the bylaw struck down, but alas, as of the time of writing there has still been no change.

In every corner of the world, from small villages to cosmopolitan North American and European metropolises, folks are permitted to keep a few backyard chickies, but not here. Not yet. So, in being so public, I am really going out on a limb, but I do it gladly, in the hope that it brings change.

It's exhausting living a life of crime!

that left the most lasting mark on me. I never stopped wanting chickens again: through college, office work and years of apartment living, it was out of the question, but I *longed* for a flock of my own. I was *that* urbanite, sitting in front of her computer until late into the night looking at pictures of coops, exotic breeds, hens, roosters, impossibly sweet and fluffy baby chicks—um, your basic chicken porn.

I read and learned, dreamed and planned for the day I'd bring my chickens home to roost. Until then, I could always garden, and I did. Oh, it was a lush garden! Soft, cool areas of grass for lying on, edged by wide swaths of wild, tall perennials and self-sowing annuals tumbling out of control—my own little English cottage garden right in the heart of the city.

I planted my veggies in tidy rows, paths of old bricks I'd found set in between; volunteer echinacea, monarda, gooseneck loosestrife and morning glory added colour and enticed pollinators and hummingbirds. At the height of summer, I could hide myself from the world behind tall, tangled masses of pinks, whites, reds, purples and greens . . . and then the chickens came.

My chicken fixation had been reaching a crescendo. I was getting frantic; the cravings were bad. So when the last impediment, a stick-in-the-mud boyfriend, got the heck out of my way, I did it. I went in search of my first flock and brought home rescued ex-battery hens, or ex-bats: two goofy Leghorns and a Rhode Island Red. One of the Leghorns was blind, so I named her Helen, as in Keller. The other was her support and they stuck together, so she became Annie Sullivan, natch! The red? Ginger.

Every season the hens teach me something new about chicken-keeping, gardening, compromising and enjoying the moment amidst the impermanence of life. And speaking of impermanence, while he didn't live to see it, I know Father would have felt right at home in my garden, my coop and my kitchen, complete with my own feathered menagerie of strays.

The way I see it, hen-keeping is a natural extension of the kitchen and garden; it's a symbiotic relationship as old as agriculture between human, hen and plants. In the peak of summer when my ladies are laying well and the garden is in major production mode, I will pop outside my back door, collect a couple of eggs—sometimes still warm from the hen—then visit the garden to see what's ripe and ready. I've made complete meals from five-minute "market trips" into the garden, feeling terribly pleased with myself and grinning like an idiot the whole time.

It's been said in a number of ways by a many folk throughout time: "hunger is the best sauce." I love that old adage, but would like to add a sprinkling of satisfaction and a dash of self-sufficiency. That stuff's damn tasty!

About This Book . . . and Me

I am a hen-keeper, gardener and professional cook. I'm not an avian veterinarian and I'm not a horticulturist. And I don't like to use the word "chef"; I prefer to reserve that title for folks who head up commercial kitchens, but yes, I have cooked professionally since 1998. And, for that matter, I've gardened professionally but have always shared garden, culinary and chicken advice freely—for the love of it.

All of this to say, my humble little book does not contain the last word on gardening or cooking or even on chicken-keeping. It contains only my word. I've loved and lived these activities for most of my years and learned a thing or three through trial and error, loss and triumph. My goal with this collection of anecdotes, advice, recipes and reminiscences is to entertain, inspire, inform and, with luck, lead you down the garden path . . . all the way to the coop and back into the kitchen, with a new or renewed passion for growing, raising and cooking your own amazing food.

YOU'VE GOTTA BREAK A FEW EGGS TO MAKE AN OMELETTE

about the recipes

My father used to say there's nothing new under the sun. He didn't live to see tiny hand-held computers, which seem pretty darn new to me, but then again, he most likely would have hauled out some morsel of history that showed Leonardo da Vinci had sketched it out centuries ago. My point is simply that some of the recipes in this book are age-old classic preparations. Many I've added a personal twist to, but there are some that just don't need the likes of me fiddling with them—they are perfect as they are—made with backyard eggs, of course!

As for the size of eggs: when recipes call for them, it's generally assumed large, and that goes for this collection too. If you're using store-bought or other graded eggs, that's easy to do. But if you're cooking with your ladies' own, the sizes may vary quite a bit. While it's fairly safe to assume that a standard-sized hen will lay large eggs, defined in North America as about 2 oz (60 g), vintage scales that you can use to weigh them are all over the internet for purchase and pretty new ones with an old-timey look are available at farm-supply shops.

When I call for butter, I cook and bake with salted; I like a little salt. If you don't, feel free to use unsalted.

Wherever and whenever possible, I have used organic dairy—and hope you will too!

When I call for fine sea salt, I just mean a fine grain as opposed to coarse, *not* fancy and expensive.

Unless otherwise indicated, flour is all-purpose.

OPPOSITE, CLOCKWISE FROM TOP: relaxing with a book of hens (DG); thrift store find—a vintage rooster spoon stand (DG); Baby in the run (DG).

And, though I should think this goes without saying, I will say it anyway; in fact, I will beg you: please, please, please do not use factory-farmed eggs. Even if you only use the odd couple in a cake mix, please choose cage-free.

I'd like to suggest that before making any recipe, read it all the way through once. Why? I've learned that if you don't, you might be surprised by an instruction down the road.

Above all, I hope this book will help to get you cooking and creating with eggs season by garden season. I hope it will hatch a few new ideas, perhaps? There's no need to order potentially unhealthy takeout when an inexpensive, delicious, filling, nutrient-dense dinner is just a few eggs and a handful of herbs away. Yes, eggs for dinner. Heck, how about my Sweet Lingonberry Jam Omelette (page 36)! Why not?

SIGNE LANGFORD PHOTO

5

spring

THE SPRING CHICKEN AND GARDEN

THE EGG: SPRING RECIPES

the spring chicken and garden

Urban hen-keeping is sweeping North America—again. Throughout history, households from royalty to peasantry have kept chickens for eggs and meat. During World War II, Canadian, American and British citizens were encouraged by their governments to keep hens. Much like planting a victory garden, it was an act of patriotism and a way everyone could contribute to the war effort. Today's renaissance of the backyard flock is driven by concerns over food security, animal welfare and a demand for healthy food. Plus, chickens are fun!

And there is no greater fun than sharing your garden with a chicken; and truly, is there a more exciting time of year than spring? My mind races with plans, expectations and to-do lists. Garden centres start popping up on grocery store parking lots, placing temptation on every corner: seeds and seedlings, new gadgets to play with, bags of goodies to add to the soil. I do not *need* another pair of gloves, and yet, and yet . . .

The sun shines brighter inside the coop, or is it the angle of it that lights up all the nooks and crannies that the weak winter light had ignored? Now I see it needs cleaning and a new coat of whitewash. This is the time of year—April and May in southern Ontario, my part of the world—when I become ruthless about taking "me days," unplugging and disappearing into my world of warming soil, melting ice and swelling buds. The birdsong is louder, love is in the air—the chickadees are singing a new song now, their come-hither "feee-beeee"—and I feel born again in my new boots.

My happiness is outdone only by the birds, squirrels and, of course, my ladies. For them, spring means a return to the sheer hedonistic pleasure of being a hen, of sprawling in sunbeams, rolling around in warming earth and hunting for juicy grubs.

And as robust as my garden is—rushing back after the brutal cold and greyness of a northern winter—it is a fragile thing too, especially with ravenous hens about.

A CHICKEN—OR THREE—IN EVERY GARDEN

It requires a little give and take, some compromise including living through the occasional disappointment and even the odd disaster, but hens and plants can survive and even thrive in each other's company. Adding a few hens to a garden creates a naturally healthy and balanced ecosystem, and trust me, you'll wonder how you ever got along without them.

File under Be Careful What You Wish For . . .
I wanted chickens. Big time. And, to be honest, I

Peanut, a bantam Cochin, helping herself to a nibble or two from the herb garden. Thyme was her favourite.

didn't even consider how they would impact my garden. I wasn't even thinking about fresh eggs. I just missed having hens in my life: the clucking, the goofiness, that unique companionable time in the backyard.

The comfy green grass was the first to go. Grass is hen heroin. Next went the tasty perennials. Then the herbs—and without a fence my veggie patch didn't stand a chance.

Like a mantra, I told myself over and over that it was worth it; I'd remind myself and anyone who noticed the shocking holes and gaps in my once-spectacular garden that the ladies were merely upcycling my pretty flowers and juicy tomatoes into the most delicious eggs ever. Well, it was true. Still, every time the breeze carried the strong aroma of basil or monarda to my nose, my heart would break a little as I wondered which of my girls was feasting now—*pre-seasoning, you little monster*, I'd think to myself!

I've had my hens since 2009, and in this time I've learned to compromise, shift the expectations I once held of my garden and create a garden the ladies and I can all enjoy. And we do, mostly without incident.

TALL FENCES MAKE GOOD NEIGHBOURS

The coop will keep hens safe at night, but during the day it's the neighbours and your precious plants that need protecting. You'll need to install fences—or other barriers, permanent or temporary—depending on the season and growth stage of a plant or area. Clear plastic tents, cloches and plant collars (even makeshift), netting, chicken

could have used this advice back when . . .

If you have a lush green lawn and would like to keep it that way, I've learned—a little late in the game—that there are ways to limit the destruction.

- Never feed the girls on the lawn. Eating leads to scratching. Scratching leads to no grass. Enough said.

- Or, if you're up for the extra work, put your ladies on a rotating schedule of lawn occupation: this simply requires a movable fencing system that's easy to set up and take down. I've known hen-keepers who have managed to have both chickens and the green, green grass of home by carefully managing where the birds are allowed to be and for how long. The area needed and time allowable for each space really depends on how many hens there are and if they are voracious grass eaters. This is a learn-on-the-job situation!

- For protecting grass, some folks swear by hens with feathered feet—Cochin, Brahma, Faverolles, Langshan, Sultan and Silkie . . . though I've got to say, I've had both a bantam Cochin and a Silkie, and if they didn't scratch as much as the others, I couldn't tell. They're just as busy with their beaks, and adorable!

the art of living with chickens

When her little flock arrived, hen-keeper and *The Art of Doing Stuff* blogger Karen Bertelsen knew nothing about chickens and even less about gardening with them. "I was taken in by all the romantic visions on Pinterest of chickens roaming freely through beautiful gardens with pea-gravel paths, so I let my chickens roam. My slate backyard was quickly covered in chicken crap, which meant so were my shoes, which meant so were the floors in my house. Also, they ate every single hosta in some sort of chicken frenzy. I didn't even see them do it. One minute I had 20 hostas, the next minute I just had a bunch of fat chickens. So at that moment I built an iron gate leading into the coop so I could still watch the chickens but they couldn't eat my greenery and then poop it out all over my backyard. These people who say chickens will eat all the bugs in your vegetable garden neglect to mention they also eat all the vegetables in your vegetable garden."

wire and branches will keep beaks and claws at bay temporarily. Attaching a mister to the hose does two things: waters and keeps hens away.

For more permanent barriers, chicken wire, wire mesh and traditional wooden fences are effective; just make sure you don't leave any gaps hens can squeeze through or under. Even a fat hen can jam herself—one wing at a time—through not much more than 5 inches (12.5 cm). Banties, even less.

In open areas, try laying down a layer of chicken wire or hardware cloth (wire mesh) over a recently seeded section, or on top of a spot where perennials will be making an appearance, then cover it up with soil. Use ground staples to anchor it and bend all sharp staple edges down toward the ground, so no feet get cut. This will stop scratching and dust bathing.

In Toronto, chicken activist Lorraine Johnson (author of *City Farmer: Adventures in Urban Food Growing*) was one of the first folks I encountered in the urban hen underground. Sounds so cloak-and-dagger, doesn't it? At the time—six years ago or so—she was really breaking some ground for the rest of us. She was also right out there at the leading edge of the hen-garden learning curve: "I had some hen-garden clashes in the early days. I believed all the people who said that chickens and gardens were great for each other. Which is true, to a degree! Chicken manure is fantastic. As is the way that hens eat insects and aerate the soil. But I made the mistake of letting them run around the whole garden, instead of just a fenced-off section, and they ate everything in sight. Now I have them in an enclosed area that is quite roomy but also leaves the rest of my garden protected." Another détente reached.

YOU'RE GROUNDED!—CLIPPING YOUR HEN'S WINGS

Another way to keep hens where you want them is to clip their wings. A hen with all her flight feathers may not glide like an eagle, but it's pretty impressive just how far and high a scared or determined yardbird can go—I've had to lure the odd hen out of a tree or down from a seven-foot fence. But a chicken with one wing clipped can only hop and flap; just enough to get around her perches, or yank a sandwich out of your hand—you've been warned.

My friend James, a veterinarian technician, gives us a step-by-step demonstration of wing clipping:

These are the flight feathers; with the tips gone, even on just one wing, a standard hen won't be able to fly the coop. Banties are light enough to require both wings be clipped.

Clipping doesn't hurt, it's like getting our hair cut. But a hen's pride does suffer; she knows she's vulnerable to predation now, so give her some extra love and treats!

Don't clip too close to the actual wing; leave a good couple of inches of feather. And don't be surprised if she's a bit clumsy for a while; she needs to relearn how high she can jump and her balance will be a slightly off for a bit.

mangel beets—a new old crop for chickens

The mangel beet (*Beta vulgaris*) was once a common crop raised as food or fodder specifically for livestock. It grows to massive proportions—up to 15, even 20 pounds!—with tall greens, and is making a comeback, with several seed houses selling this heritage breed.

Although slow to mature (from 70 to 100 days), mangel beets store well and provide the gals with great winter snacking and activity: come winter, try hanging one up in the run.

WHEN YOUR BACKYARD IS CHICKEN SCRATCH

I've already warned you about what chickens can do to grass. Think hippies at Woodstock: they'll hoover it up. If you're not too attached to your putting-green lawn, go ahead and let your flock do its worst, then exchange the lawn for other ground covers: pea gravel, chips, mulch, pavers. Introducing more hard landscaping to your garden is a good idea with hens; it's damage-proof and easily hosed or swept clean.

And now is the time, as you embark on the big spring planting, to lock gates, staple up wire, run fences, drape plastic sheeting and set out your cloches. The ladies will be keeping an eagle eye on you as you putter—believe me, they don't miss a beat! If you bend down and so much as touch the soil, move a rock, reach out to grab a pitchfork, they *will* see it and they *will* be on that very patch of ground in seconds—as fast as their drumsticks can carry them—pecking and scratching. It's adorable and makes it impossible to get a darn thing done!

I suppose some hard-hearted Hannahs might lock up their ladies while they garden but I couldn't bear it; gardening is about a million times more fun with my crew of helpers. They're

I replaced my grass with pea gravel—it looks gorgeous (especially after a rain), the hens enjoy scratching through it for sprouts and bugs, and it just requires a raking every now and then.

Don't discard those broken pots; they make great hen guards for tempting plants!

the bottom line

If you don't want the ladies to "help" you with your gardening, you can't let them see you planting. And this seems like as good a time as any to point this out: if you don't like being watched intently, through windows, doors or as you go about your business in the garden, hens are not for you. If you don't enjoy being followed around constantly, you know, just to see if you are possibly headed toward the biggest cache of cutworms in the history of the world, then hens are not for you. With hens you will, as the song says, never walk alone.

essential when turning the beds, though there will be some delays, as hens slide into freshly dug holes or perch on the tines of a pitchfork for advantage. And yes, there will be collateral damage as they gobble up benevolent earthworms, but they will also wolf down every nasty grub, slug and potato bug you uncover. So, it's a reasonable trade-off that ultimately works out in the garden's favour.

It's when we add fragile seedlings or our beloved perennials start poking their heads out of the ground that our garden is at its most vulnerable. This is when it's particularly important to protect anything you don't want your ladies to destroy. Don't let them near it until it is *very* well established with a root system that can survive a bit of abuse.

Clear as a Bell

When it comes to safeguarding vulnerable plants, cloches are your new best friends. And not just the expensive bell jars most gardeners covet for protecting transplants, seedlings or a beloved specimen. Whenever I go to a second-hand shop or visit a garage sale, I put my cloche goggles on: if it's the right size, made of clear plastic or glass, is open at one end or even both, as far as I'm concerned it's a cloche. I've used glass lampshades, trash cans, vases and hurricane-lamp flues. It's a good idea to start amassing a collection before you introduce hens to your garden.

Going to Spot

Seems all chickens like to eat tiny speck-type things or little balls, beads or, ahem, one's pearls; that's three of my pearl studs at last count down Miss Vicky's gullet. And this is why potting soil is a hen magnet. The vermiculite and perlite just beg to be eaten! And, of course, once the top layer is devoured, they're going to scratch up your freshly planted posies looking for more.

This is my only true cloche; I use vases, glass pendant lampshades, punch bowls, acrylic trash cans, flues, anything clear and the right shape to protect small plants from my tiny dinos.

To prevent this, I like to dress or cover my potting soil with a good layer of pea gravel; they have no interest in eating this, I think it looks nice and it helps hold moisture in. You could also add a layer of plain topsoil to hide the tantalizing hen bait.

ALL-SHE-CAN-EAT SALAD BAR

Okay, let's just say, for the sake of argument, that you want backyard hens but do *not* wish to share your whole lawn and garden with them. Let's say—for some incomprehensible reason— you have an aversion to chicken poop on your garden furniture, patio stones, shoes, bum (you are going to sit on chicken poop), and you plan on giving your ladies a lovely spacious run. You need to know that if there is anything growing in that space it will be no more. So, might I suggest a protected growing area where you can sow seeds—beet, radish, lettuce, kale—and keep them safe from pecks and scratches until they've grown

SIGNE LANGFORD PHOTO

into a beak-watering salad bar? There are a few ways to do this, and it comes down to available space, light and your handyman skill level:

containers: If you have very little space or the run isn't sunny enough for planting, pots are a perfect solution. This way, you can grow in the sun and move the container into the run when it's full of green goodness. If you do seed it inside the run, make sure to cover it with a cloche of some sort—something solid and heavy enough or fastened down so that the girls can't push it off, because they *will* try!

straw bale with cover: This one's easy but requires a bit of room. Make a square out of four bales of straw. Dump some topsoil or triple mix into the centre, and then seed, water and cover with an old window. When the veggies are as big as you'd like them to be for the ladies, remove the window and pull away one of the bales. The ladies will rush in like teenage girls at a One Direction concert! Bonus: you'll use that straw for bedding in the end, so it's a very eco-friendly solution.

wooden raised bed with cover: You need a bit of skill with a hammer and saw, but essentially this is the same as the straw bale. If you make one long bed attached to an inner wall or fence inside the run, you might want to divide it into a few independent sections, each with its own lid (window) so that you can offer veggies to the ladies one section at a time. This way, you can keep it growing all the time—staggered—and never be without.

THE ULTIMATE HEN HERB GARDEN

Hen-keeper extraordinaire, author and blogger Lisa Steele lives on a bucolic farm in Virginia, where she tends to her flock of chickens and ducks naturally, with healing herbs and foods.

"Culinary herbs are easy to grow and have amazing health benefits for both you and your chickens, helping to keep them healthy naturally, without the use of antibiotics or medications. Culinary herbs are perfectly safe to use around the chickens, so there's no worry about any being toxic or harmful. However, I do usually feed the herbs free-choice so my hens can pick and choose and eat what they want, as much or as little as they want. I put fresh herbs in the nesting boxes to calm setting hens, repel insects and rodents, and make the coop smell nice. I brew herbal tea for our baby chicks and offer them fresh chopped herbs to give them a good start in life. It's so easy to toss a variety of herbs into your brooder, coop and nesting boxes any time you trim your herb plants."

I asked Lisa to imagine a dream garden of all the best herbs to plant around the coop. Some keep pests at bay, some are medicinal, some are nutritious and delicious, and some are so aromatic they out-scent hen poop!

chamomile: Chamomile is a great addition to the nesting boxes since it is reputed to kill lice and mites and is calming to laying hens. A natural antiseptic, it makes a great eye rinse or wash to soothe inflamed or injured eyes when brewed into a tea and then cooled.

lavender: Naturally soothing, lavender can help calm laying and broody hens. Used in the nesting boxes, either fresh or dried, the leaves and flower buds provide some nice aromatherapy, and act as an insect repellent—which is important, since the warm, dark area in the box and under

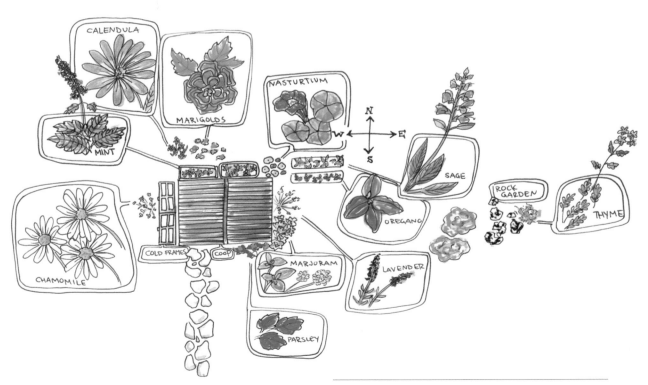

A lovely coop herb garden filled with all of Lisa Steele's favourite healing herbs for happy and healthy hens.

the hen can become a breeding ground for para-sites. As the hen pecks at the fragrant herb as she sits, lavender also increases circulation.

marigolds and calendula: Marigolds are insect repellent and anti-inflammatory, a source of carotenes, lutein and lycopene, and help repair skin tissue and aid in blood-vessel growth. The petals contain xanthophyll, which results in vibrant orange egg yolks, as well as nice dark orange legs and feet. The leaves and stems can cause mouth irritation, so I harvest only the pet-als. While our chickens will sometimes eat them fresh, I find it works better to dry and crush the petals and mix them into the layer feed.

marjoram: Marjoram does double duty for our chickens. The fresh or dried leaves in the nest-ing boxes work as a laying stimulant and increase blood circulation for sitting hens when they ingest them. Marjoram is also an anti-inflammatory and

decongestant, so it has benefits when added to the layer feed in a dried form. My chickens also love fresh marjoram leaves, so I feed them free-choice in season.

mint: Mint is another herb that does double duty. It is a natural rodent and insect repellent, so I use fresh mint leaves in the coop regularly to help keep out field mice, flies and other bugs. Mint also works to lower body temperature naturally, so I often freeze the leaves with berries, peas or corn kernels in water in ice cube trays and offer the frozen ice pops to the chickens to help cool them off in the summer.

nasturtium: Nasturtium has been used as a natural wormer for years in livestock keeping, and is also a laying stimulant. I feed them the leaves, seeds and petals all summer when my gar-den is overflowing with this easy-to-grow edible flower.

oregano: Oregano is being studied as a natu-ral antibiotic and thought to help combat many of the common avian illnesses. I steep fresh or dried oregano leaves in warm water to make tea for my baby chicks in the brooder to help build their immune systems and fight off any pathogens

LEFT: *Fresh Eggs Daily* blogger Lisa Steele with Violet, her Lavender Orpington. RIGHT: Confessions of a marigold hater: I've never been a fan. Don't like the 1970s orange and yellow, don't like the ruffled flowers, can't stand the smell—but then I found these! Deep burnt orange, understated single bloom, and yes, they still stink.

they might encounter. I also add dried oregano to my chickens' daily layer feed and offer my flock fresh oregano leaves straight from the garden. Oregano is especially effective when combined with cinnamon, so if a chicken is ailing, mixing some oregano and cinnamon into their feed or a tea can be beneficial.

parsley: Parsley is extremely nutritious and my chickens love it. I toss them fresh parsley from the garden and dry the leaves to add to their daily layer feed. In addition to its wonderful vitamins, it's a laying stimulant!

sage: Sage, traditionally often paired with chicken dishes, is thought to help combat salmonella. I like to dry the leaves, which also have antioxidant properties, and add them crushed to my chickens' daily layer feed.

thyme: Thyme has powerful respiratory and antibacterial properties. Since chickens are so susceptible to breathing problems due to their extremely complicated respiratory systems, I add dried thyme to their daily layer feed.

SPRING CLEANING THE COOP

Sounds crazy, I know, but one of my favourite spring chores is mucking out the coop and run. Of course, I conduct micro-cleanings every day: I use a wide plaster knife to scrape up the day's deposit of poop from inside the coop, rake out heavily soiled bedding, and dust and spray with pest-controlling stuff such as diatomaceous earth, mite spray and neem oil. But the big spring cleanup means the coop is stripped out, hosed down, treated and medicated, and re-whitewashed with a coat of watered-down primer. I even hang some new nest-box curtains. And that's not just being saccharine—hens like a little privacy when they're doing their egg-laying business. Even some of the less brutal egg factories are supplying their

garden gold from the chicken coop

"Chicken poop, when mixed with the straw in their bedding, is the absolute *best* compost anyone could ask for," says hen-keeper Karen Bertelsen. "It's the perfect mix of browns and greens that compost needs to hot-compost. If I make a big pile and turn it every other day I can turn chicken poop and straw into compost in less than a month—it's brilliant! I then use that compost on my off-limits vegetable garden. I put it in planting holes, side-dress plants and make compost tea" (see Hen Poop Tea, page 127).

birds with curtained-off areas to lay. It's in a hen's DNA to want to feel safe and hidden when laying or setting.

The bedding I pull out from the coop is dry but poopy, and the stuff I rake up from the run is wet in places and also poopy, but heavy, compacted, decomposing and, man oh man, does it ever stink! The smell is one I recognize as the result of imbalance, of anaerobic decomposition, so I'm confident that very soon after I've moved it out into the air and sun, the deadly smell will go. This temporarily stinky stuff is gold; rich and already halfway to soil, and once spread on the garden, it breaks down the rest of the way in one summer. I space out where I dump the gunk, and though incomprehensible to me, the ladies love it. They'll dig through the horrid stuff, picking out tasty little nuggets of sprouting grain or bugs, spreading it out for me in the process. Thanks, ladies!

Birds of a Feather

The sparrows hang around while I muck out the coop. They're waiting for feathers. It's just delightful to watch them swoop in and pluck one from the ground, or even from mid-air. I love imagining the soft, warm nests their babes will hatch into, courtesy of my ladies. The boldest birds will inch ever closer to grab a feather near my feet or even one held between my fingers. And, if a hen happens to be moulting, the sparrows will follow her around like a personal cleanup crew, retrieving every feather she sheds. Sometimes an overzealous bird can't stand the wait, and will pluck any feather that appears to be flapping too loosely for its own good—right out of a napping hen. *Yoink!*

Better Henhouse Keeping

I've said it before and I'll say it again: a chicken coop is outside, somewhat open to the elements, and often visited by wild birds and the occasional rodent, so I really don't think it's possible to keep it 100 percent pest-free. It's simply about control and management. In Minnie Rose Lovgreen's charming guide, *Recipe for Raising Chickens*, she suggests slathering crankcase grease on the perches. Sage advice, as it will suffocate any critters lurking in cracks and crevices. But slippery? Yes. And if, like me, you are a hen-snuggler, the resulting greasy feet will be hazardous to your

wardrobe. So I put oils—neem, vegetable, mineral—in tucked-away places, and use pest-control powders and sprays on the rest of the coop and the ladies. Look for non-toxic, natural, herbal kinds for day-to-day maintenance. But, if confronted with a serious infestation, go for the big guns, and that means chemical pesticides and sometimes veterinary pharmaceuticals available through farm and agricultural supply shops and by mail order where import laws permit.

TASTY OR TOXIC?

Before introducing hens to a garden, do your homework: which plants are toxic to chickens, which are medicinal and which are just tasty eats?

The list of toxic plants is long and not entirely unanimous, so I've simply noted the most commonly planted or surprising ones here; you can seek out a more comprehensive list by consulting a few chicken-keeping websites. In my own experience, I've noticed some of my hens feasting on supposedly toxic plants to no apparent ill effect. Of course, I can't see if liver damage has taken place, but I've discovered my ladies on numerous occasions plucking leaves from bleeding hearts—supposedly a real no-no—and living to cluck another day. In fact, once you start researching by visiting poultry-keeping message boards and chat rooms and reading books, you'll soon see that one hen can eat something considered toxic while another cannot.

In a few cases, small doses of some toxic plants are actually medicinal, and hens seem to know when to stop eating the potentially scary stuff. Besides, nature tends to make poisonous plants taste very bitter, and that's a real deterrent, especially for spoiled chickens used to fresh baby arugula and sweet corn niblets.

there's one in every flock: the snuggler

Some are born that way and some have to be convinced that cuddling with a human is a good idea. Get a hen young enough and spend enough time holding her—stroking her chin, giving ear-patch scratches and breathing warm air onto her neck feathers—and she'll soon decide that spending time in your lap or arms or, like Baby, wrapped up in a coat or shirt, is just grand!

Busted! Big Mamma (left), and indeed all the ladies, enjoy a little nibble of bleeding heart (right) every now and then. It's not something I encourage, but I don't discourage it either.

I should also say that I've not tested all these plants out . . . for obvious reasons! So while some here seem harmless to me, I've included them because they are on many cautionary lists. And better safe than sorry, right?

avocado: All parts of the plant are poisonous to hens, including the fruit, pit and skin.

azalea, rhododendron, mountain laurel: All beautiful and, sadly, all very poisonous to animals.

beans (castor, fava, scarlet runner and others): I plant a fair number of beans and the leaves hold no interest for the girls; bumblebees, on the other hand, *love* scarlet runners!

bleeding heart: Despite warnings from others, the shady spots in my garden are full of it and the ladies find it delicious; so far, not one has keeled over from a beakful.

bloodroot: I had this delicate little North American native flower in my garden for years. It was the very first shoot up out of the ground in spring, and while the ladies never took a bite, they did scratch the heck out of it.

blue-green algae: Only a concern if the ladies have access to a pond or other water feature. Frankly, I'd worry more about them drowning than eating the algae.

boxwood and privet: I have boxwood in my garden and they've never shown any interest in it; must not be tasty.

bulb and rhizome flowers (arum and calla lily, amaryllis, autumn crocus, daffodil, hyacinth, iris, narcissus, tulip): The squirrels cured me of trying to enjoy bulbs years ago, but I see their appeal—just plant where the ladies don't go.

burdock: So surprising! The root is edible for humans (in fact, it's a delicacy in Japan), and some hen-keepers swear by its medicinal properties.

buttercup: Plants in the *Ranunculus* genus, from the innocent buttercup to the showiest border perennials, are deadly when consumed fresh, but taste unbearably bitter and cause blistering in the mouth, so are usually left alone.

cacao: While none of us north of Mexico can actually grow the stuff, it bears mentioning that chocolate is highly toxic to most animals.

cherry tree: The leaves, branches and pits are the problem, but they love the fruit! My clever girls will eat all the tasty flesh from around the pit and leave it. The pit contains small amounts of cyanogenic acids—yup, that's cyanide. It's in other stone fruits too—plums, peaches, apricots and almonds, as well as in the seeds of apples and pears. But the amount is tiny, so don't lose it if your ladies swallow a couple of seeds or pits; they'd have to chew them first to release the poison and, as we all know, hens' teeth are rare!

clematis: Clematis of every variety climbs all over my garden and the ladies are completely disinterested.

creeping myrtle or periwinkle: Despite being known as the "Flower of Death," it's rarely lethal for pets and livestock. Still, since it's a creeper, the girls would spend more time picking at it than is good for them, so I avoid it.

delphinium: Too bad; this is one of the prettiest plants in the border, but a real no-no.

elderberry: This is surprising, as some hens can and do eat it without any issues.

I've seen clematis on the toxic-for-chickens list, but my ladies have never shown even the slightest interest, which is lucky for me, since I love them. This variety is 'Elsa Spath'.

foxglove: The source of the heart medicine digitalis, I imagine one nibble too many could lead to a heart attack in a hen's little heart.

holly, ivy, mistletoe and poinsettia: Avoid all the Christmas plants!

honeysuckle and jasmine: Now that is disappointing—I love the sweet smell and so do the hummingbirds!

hydrangea: I have a couple in my garden and the ladies leave it alone. So far, so good; it must taste terrible!

jack-in-the-pulpit, lady slipper and other orchids: They even *look* menacing in an evil sexy-princess kind of way.

juniper: And yet there'd be no gin without it!

lily of the valley: This pretty and beautifully scented shade lover will make humans sick too.

lobelia: Only a minor worry—the species is more medicinal than poisonous and used in folk medicine still to this day.

marijuana or hemp: Not only is it ill-advised to grow this plant for legal reasons, it's also important not to smoke it near your hens. The same goes for cigarettes. A carelessly discarded cigarette butt or joint is toxic to hens and could start a fire in a tinder-dry, straw-filled henhouse.

poppies: I'd play it safe with this one and not plant any variety. Too bad; they are lovely.

milkweed: While the thick white sap is toxic, the plant is super-important to the survival of the monarch butterfly so do plant it, just not where your hens spend time.

morning glory: My ladies have never shown an ounce of interest in the morning glory that self-sows all over my garden fences. The seeds are a known hallucinogen: I've watched squirrels feast on the tender leading tendrils in the spring and dry black seeds in the fall, and

spinach? what the . . . really?

Don't feed the ladies too much spinach. And the same goes for sorrel and mountain (or narrow-leaf) dock. It all comes down to a substance in these greens—oxalic acid—that has the pesky habit of binding with calcium and making it hard for the ladies to absorb it. And with all that shell-building, the girls need as much calcium as they can get their beaks on.

Oh, and by the way, this goes for us too. But the good news is that all it takes to set things right is a little kitchen chemistry. Enjoy your spinach with a vinaigrette made with apple-cider vinegar, which will break down the oxalic acid to let your body take up the calcium. (That's great for us, but I know my ladies don't care for the sour taste of vinegar.)

the physical comedy that follows is something I should sell tickets for!

mushrooms and fungus: You really can't control where mushrooms will pop up, and even when I've tossed the ladies delicious leftovers containing mushrooms, they simply eat around them. Smart girls!

nettles: I love eating them; so delicious and full of vitamins. Of course, they hurt like heck to touch unless blanched, cooked or dried, but toxic? That's a real surprise to me and again you won't find a unanimous opinion on this subject.

oak tree leaves and acorns: Leaves and acorns are toxic to certain animals, as they contain large amounts of tannic acid (like the tannins found in red wine and tea), while critters such as squirrels and the famous acorn-fed pata negra swine of Spain can eat acorns with impunity. Even weirder, the flavour is so enticing to the

shades of danger

The nightshade (Solanaceae) family spreads far and wide, with cousins springing up in gardens and the wild around the world. In North America, we grow many members of this tasty but somewhat toxic family of common vegetables—tomato, eggplant, ground cherry, tomatillo, potato, pepper, Chinese lantern, goji berry—as well as such ornamentals as nicotiana, brugmansia (datura or angel's trumpet), petunias and henbane (well, that figures!), to name but 12 of its 2,700 or so species.

You've most likely come across bittersweet and deadly nightshade vines, and vacillated about pulling them out or not. The foliage is dark green and vigorous, and the little purple flowers are kind of cute, as are the tiny red berries, but it's so toxic that I say yank it! The poison in all nightshade members renders the leaves and stems very bitter, so my girls have never gone for the foliage of any of these plants. Now the fruit is quite another thing. Between the girls, squirrels and raccoons, planting ground cherries, tomatoes and eggplant is an exercise in heartache . . . for me. As for the thieves? They seem perfectly fine.

very animals it is toxic to that they return again and again, no matter how sick it makes them. Curiouser and curiouser.

oleander: Toxic in large quantities, but certain animals and humans are more susceptible than others.

rhubarb leaves: Here's another one of those mysteries. My hens *do* eat the toxic leaves—never very much, but they do take a bite every now and then—and they've been fine afterwards.

sweet pea and lupine: Both members of the legume family, these pretty perfumed nitrogen-fixers contain neurotoxins, but a hen would have to consume a lot to become ill.

virginia creeper: It may well be toxic, as many sources claim, but it's everywhere around my house and the ladies pay it no mind.

wisteria: So very pretty and mostly out of reach, so I don't worry.

yew: The needles and berries are poisonous, but I have an affection for the evergreen ever since I read that it's also toxic to cancer cells. So, I grow one, and you can too, just not where the girls go.

EASTER EGGS, NATURALLY

My sweet Easter Egger, Noella, lays the prettiest blue-green eggs—they come out ready for Easter brunch! But colouring your own Easter eggs is fun and if you've got some kids around to entertain, it's *de rigueur!* I think artificial food colourings are kind of brash, and much prefer the softer, subtler hues natural plants and spices give to eggshells. If garden space permits, why not grow some of the plants you'll need to naturally colour your girls' eggs? Here are plants you can grow yourself for dye:

beets: Those good old dark red ones impart the best colour. The leafy tops are tasty for human or hen, too.

blueberries: These fruit-bearing shrubs are fantastic for birds, bees, humans and hens, while the berries give a soft blue hue to white eggs and make blue eggs bluer!

blackberries and raspberries: The fruit is extremely tasty and a great natural dye too; the leaves are medicinal for humans and hens alike. In spring, when canes are leafing out, supply some protection as that's when foliage is most tempting to hens (see Tall Fences Make Good Neighbours, page 9).

Subtly gorgeous Easter eggs in soft and mottled shades of Madras, gunmetal and russet.

purple or red cabbage: Use the tough outer leaves for dyeing—if you've got any left over from the late fall harvest—and keep the centre for eating. White eggs will turn a soft red.

yellow onions: The boiled skins give off a pinkish-red colour to white-shelled eggs.

saffron crocus: This fall-blooming true crocus can be grown as far north as Zone 5. Plant it out of reach of hens; it's considered toxic for them. Harvest the stigma for drying and turning into saffron threads; use in cooking and for lending eggs a soft yellowish red.

spinach: Boil up and mush spinach for a soft pastel green.

But until that Easter Egg Garden is flourishing, the grocery store has everything you need to make pretty, soft and subtle eggs this Easter:

DYE STAPLES
- Vegetable oil
- White vinegar

DYE POSSIBILITIES
- Beets, beet juice or leftover brine-pickled beets
- Blueberries, blackberries, cranberries, strawberries and raspberries
- Coffee
- Oranges, for the peels
- Red or purple cabbage
- Red wine
- Saffron and safflower
- Soy sauce
- Spinach
- Tea, black or green
- Turmeric
- Yellow cooking onions, for the skins

Let's Dye Some Eggs!

It's easy to dye beautiful backyard eggs with natural colourings—spices, foods and even home-grown herbs and vegetables—but the effect is much more subtle than you might be accustomed to, and if your ladies lay only brown eggs, you won't see much change. Best to start with white eggs, and if this means you have to rush right out to get yourself a lovely rescued Leghorn, well then, so be it!

Before you get started, it's important to wash backyard eggs to remove the bloom, as it will repel the dye a fair bit. Natural dyes result in softer, subtler colours, so don't expect Day-Glo orange; think pretty pastels.

Add 1 tablespoon (15 mL) white vinegar to each cup (250 mL) of water added to the colouring pot. Because the vinegar is an acid, it actually etches into the calcium of the shell, providing a rougher, more porous surface for the dye to soak into.

Add the colouring agent of your choice to the pot and bring to a simmer until you like the colour of the water.

Once you're happy with the colour of your water, add the raw eggs and cook, following the directions for perfect hard-boiled eggs on page 26. Don't take them out of the coloured water to cool; leave them in the dye bath for as long as you want, though after 24 hours, chances are the dye has given all it has to give.

Take the eggs out and let them drip dry on a cooling rack over a pan, old newspapers or a tea towel you don't mind getting all splattered with dye.

Once your pretty dyed eggs are perfectly dry, buff them up all shiny with a bit of vegetable oil and a dry cloth.

YES, I LEAVE MY EGGS ON THE COUNTER . . . ALL. YEAR. LONG.

Not only does it look gorgeous—as in urban-homesteading-decor-magazine-centrefold gorgeous—it also means I'm not taking up primo space in the fridge and can cook with room-temperature eggs, which I like, and which some recipes specifically call for.

Eggs—the way nature makes them—do not need to be kept cold. In most parts of the world, eggs are collected, graded, transported, sold and stored at room temperature. The reason we refrigerate eggs in North America is, I think, twofold. One, we're a germophobic society. And two, the North American egg industry has messed with nature. A hen's digestive tract and oviduct—that's the route the developing egg takes toward the vent—are separate, until just inside the vent. In other words, poop and eggs travel different highways but use the same exit ramp from the body: the vent, or cloaca. Sounds dirty, right? Sounds like a case of bad design, doesn't it? However, Mother Nature has that covered. Literally. Before the fully formed egg reaches that shared part where the two pathways come together, the hen puts something called the "bloom" on the eggshell. The bloom is a protective antibacterial coating that prevents poop bacteria from passing through the egg's porous shell and into your breakfast. So, washing eggs in water not only removes this wondrous bloom, it also allows bacteria to pass through the shell. And that's why unwashed eggs can sit out on the counter; it's also why a fresh unwashed egg with a little bit of poop stuck to it is just fine. Don't wash it with water, just wipe or scrape off the offending doo-doo with a dry rag.

And, yes, the egg industry washes their eggs in a mild bleach-and-water solution, removing the bloom and possibly allowing the bleach-water to permeate the pores of the shells, necessitating refrigeration.

Just remember that folks have been eating eggs with non-lethal results for millennia; heck, most homes didn't even have an icebox until well into the 1840s. Of course, other methods of preservation have been used over time. Century or thousand-year eggs have been produced in many parts of Asia for centuries, and lately it's come to my attention that the age-old practice of salt-preserving yolks—turning them into hard orange balls that resemble tiny mimolette cheeses—is gaining popularity amongst urban homesteaders (see Ancient Salt-Cured Yolks, page 58).

ack! there's a blood spot in my egg!

Fret not, unless there was a rooster in the henhouse the egg can't be fertilized; that little speck of red is harmless and flavourless. Sometimes a wee drop of blood is produced when the yolk leaves the hen's ovary, but it's perfectly normal: the egg is good to eat and, my dear vegetarians, it's not a potential life. Pick the spot out if it bothers you and enjoy that delicious egg from a happy hen!

there's one in every flock: the nest hog

In my flock, it's Noella, a bossy, not-too-bright Rumpless Araucana, who lays pretty blue eggs. It's my affection for her Easter eggs that has spared her being sent back to the farm from whence she came. If any of my girls is going to get us busted, it's going to be her, and all because she never learned to share, or she's terrible at math. The girls have seven nest boxes—more than enough for five hens, or so you'd think, but when any of the others go into a box to lay she'll bellow in outrage at the top of her lungs. Continuously. In and out of the coop. Up and down the ramp, poking her head through the curtains to yell at the occupant. And does she stop once the poor, harassed sitting hen exits? No. Now Miss Thing is outraged because there's an egg—*an egg*!—in *her* box. The only way to make her stop is to remove the offending object. Diva!

the egg: spring recipes

After a long, dull Canadian winter, spring is as welcome to my tummy as it is to my sunshine-deprived skin and soul. Early spring doesn't offer loads of produce from the garden, but there are certain treasures: fiddleheads, maple sap for syrup, sprouts, chives and, perhaps most thrilling of all, asparagus.

My asparagus patch is still young—the harvest would barely satisfy a hungry mouse—so as soon as I see "Ontario" replace "Mexico" or "Chile" in front of "asparagus" at the grocery store, I go a little nuts. I buy three bunches at a time—for me and me alone. The first bunch I usually cook before I've even put the rest of the groceries away. Well, I put the pan of water on and put away perishables while I wait for it to come to a boil. I'll blanch this first exquisitely fresh, tender and tasty bunch; then half the spears will go into an ice bath, the other directly onto my plate where I will roll the hot stuff around in butter and salt and stand there at the kitchen counter, surrounded by shopping bags, head back, spears going in one after another like some kind of human asparagus chipper.

The first half gone, I'm not sated just yet, but have at least pulled back from the brink of asparagus mania. Just.

The second half is now drying on a tea towel, and I'm poking around in the fridge for my jar of

SIGNE LANGFORD PHOTO

mayonnaise. And this is how I'll relish this serving; ice cold, dipped into good mayonnaise. Not necessarily homemade, but a high-quality brand made with free-run eggs and olive oil.

Now I can put the rest of my groceries away, while I consider how to prepare the other bunches. With every new bunch of Ontario asparagus I bring home, the preparations will become more elaborate—by number four, I don't mind sharing it with other flavours—and what I have found is the richness of farm- or backyard-fresh eggs goes beautifully with fresh asparagus, and I'll pair the two in many different ways until the signs read "Mexico" again.

And while I may not have fresh asparagus every day, I do always have fresh eggs, so let's cook some up!

how to boil an egg

Sounds simple, right? Water + egg + heat + time = soft-boiled or hard-boiled egg. Oh, but what about that creepy greenish tinge the yolk gets? Or whites that are rubbery or bulging through cracks? You see? There's much to consider.

HARD-BOILING: MY WAY

Here's how I make hard-boiled eggs: I start with eggs in a pot of cold water to cover. Then I bring it to a good boil.

As soon as it boils, I turn the burner off and let the pot sit there for as long as it takes to cool. Some prefer to time that last part—letting the eggs sit for 10 to 15 minutes in the hot water, then transferring them to icy-cold water to chill instantly. Either way, simple and done—and perfect!

SOFT-BOILING: METHOD 1

Soft-boiling is another beast altogether. Because timing is so important, some start the clock when the egg is lowered into already-boiling water, but then you risk cracking. It's the rapid temperature change between the fridge and the boiling water that causes the crack. I don't keep my eggs in the fridge, so they go into the water at room temperature and do not crack.

If you do keep your eggs cold, bring them up to room temperature before adding gently to the water; give them a couple of hours on the counter by the stove to warm up. And the water doesn't need to be in a high rolling boil; a gentle boil will do the trick without jostling the egg around nearly as much. Then hit the timer: 2 minutes for runny yolk and just-done white.

SOFT-BOILING: METHOD 2

Here's another way that also works: use the same method for soft-boiling as for hard. Start with eggs in cold water, bring to a boil, then cover and set aside for 2 to 3 minutes. Drain water and immediately run cold water over eggs or let them sit in icy-cold water until cooled.

No matter how they're boiled, the peeling instructions are the same: crack the shell all over on a hard surface, then roll the egg between your hands to loosen the shell. Begin peeling at the large end, and hold under cold running water to help remove the shell. See the sidebar for tips on peeling fresh eggs.

DON'T COUNT YOUR CHICKS BEFORE THEY HATCH

backyard eggs: too fresh?

When I first started with backyard eggs, I thought I'd make some devilled eggs for a party. I boiled up a bunch, picked one up, gave it a wee tap on the counter to crack the shell and started to peel. A chunk of shell, membrane and layer of egg white came away. So I checked in with the online chicken community and, sure enough, it's a classic greenhorn problem. There are plenty of opinions and tricks out there; I've tried them all and here's what works when it comes to the boiling and pretty peeling of backyard eggs.

Poke a few tiny holes in the round end of the egg before adding to a pot of cold water to boil. This might let some air out or water in, and make a separation between shell and egg.

When boiling eggs, add about 1 teaspoon (5 mL) of vinegar, or 1 tablespoon (15 mL) salt or baking soda, to a large pot of water. This softens the shell, as the acid eats through the calcium, and may help the membrane separate from the shell.

Keep aside a bowl of eggs just for hard-boiling, and let them age for about 2 weeks before cooking. Even with a little aging your backyard eggs will still taste about a thousand times better than store-bought.

One of the reasons put forth for the peeling problem is that the interior of the egg is too moist.

SIGNE LANGFORD PHOTO

Some swear by steaming, using a bamboo steamer, metal steamer, double boiler, or whatever works. Add a few inches of water to the pot; don't let the water touch the eggs. Bring to a boil and let the eggs steam for about 15 to 20 minutes.

Whether you steam or boil, as soon as the eggs are done, drain the hot water, then shake the pot around, causing the eggs to bang against the sides and each other, cracking a bit. Add cold water, pause for a few seconds, drain again, add more cold water and let sit until completely cooled. The cracks should let in some of the water, which helps to separate the membrane from the interior of the shell.

Ginger and Lizzy Borden, two ex-battery hens fully recovered and enjoying their hard-earned retirement.

essential egg recipes
done perfectly . . . my way

Cooking eggs right seems simple, but requires a gentle touch. Some chefs need only observe an applicant make an omelette to decide if they are worth hiring. If you can do justice to an egg, there may be a great cook inside you, just waiting to break out of your shell. *Sorry*.

And while it might seem as simple as boiling water, many folks mess it up: vinegary poached eggs, dried-out scrams, that creepy green halo around a hard-boiled yolk, leathery brown omelettes that taste bitter . . . but it doesn't need to be this way.

silver and gold

Is it just me or do silver spoons taste weird with eggs? Nope, it's a chemical reaction. Silver exaggerates the taste of an egg's naturally present sulphur. Stainless steel, ceramic or even wood is better. Gold is best!

SCRAMBLED

In my experience, most folks overcook scrambled eggs. Perfect scrambled eggs should be creamy and moist—a bit liquidy in spots—never the rubbery little pellets I so often see bounced onto a plate.

Here's how I make my simply wonderful scrams: keep the heat at medium or lower. Use butter and only butter, about 1 teaspoon (5 mL) or more per egg in the pan. Put the butter in first and let it melt.

CLOCKWISE FROM TOP LEFT: shirred, coddled, hard-boiled, poached, soft-boiled and devilled.

In a bowl, beat the eggs fast and furious, pumping a good amount of air into them. Father always added a shake of Tabasco but I like mine with just salt and pepper. If I happen to have some cream in the fridge, I'll add about 1 teaspoon (5 mL) for each egg before beating.

Pour the eggs into the pan, and keep it moving. Don't let it sit in one place and form a bottom or begin to brown. And always remove from the heat and get the eggs out of the pan immediately *before* it looks cooked. Believe me, the heat being retained by the pan and eggs will continue to cook them. If you've never had wet scrams before, don't be squeamish. Try it, you will love the silky texture and rich flavour. And please, please, please, don't hold back on the butter— margarine is the enemy, as is self-denial.

FRIED

For me, this is the classic. Well, over easy, that is—sunny side up is prettiest but I can't abide egg slime. Again, the key is temperature and fat. Butter is my fat of choice, but I've been known to fry an egg in bacon drippings and that's pretty nice, too. Chef Roger Mooking will sometimes fry eggs in coconut oil; if you're dressing the eggs

tip

Always rinse residual egg from dishes and utensils in cold water. Hot water simply cooks the egg and makes it stick even harder! Once it's been rinsed off in cold, then go ahead and wash as normal.

with some lovely Caribbean or Asian flavours, this makes a ton of sense.

When the eggs are as good as backyard eggs are, their flavour should shine, so butter is best. For a perfect fried egg I like high heat—that egg should sizzle when it hits the pan—and there needs to be enough butter to create a crunchy, lacy golden frill all around the edges. When the edges look crispy, flip it over, count three Mississippis and either slide or flip it yolk-up onto the plate.

Sometimes, if I've just boiled the kettle and its bottom is still scorching hot, I'll set it on top of the pan, so the heat radiating down from the kettle cooks the top of the egg. It's not touching the egg, just resting on the edges of the pan. No flipping needed and what you get is something between over easy and sunny side up; a sort of overcast egg! Another way to do overcast eggs is to fry them in unconscionable amounts of fat, so that near the end of the cooking you can tip the pan and baste the top of the yolk with a spoon until the white cooks just a titch.

CODDLED

I'd never heard this term until Mother went to the UK and came home with a collection of pretty crockery egg coddlers with shiny metal screw-tops. She'd smear the inside with gobs of butter, crack an egg or two in, sprinkle a little salt and pepper, then fasten the lid on tightly. The tops had wee loop handles that she'd use to lower the coddler into a pot of boiling water, where it would sit for several minutes. What emerged was an egg floating in warm butter—not quite steamed, not quite baked, and so much better than poached or boiled. Don't run out and spend a fortune on coddlers—just use small, squat, wide-mouth mason jars.

Bottom-Loaded Coddled Eggs: I like the idea of hiding something tasty and surprising under the eggs at the bottom of the coddler. Lots of things can work—you just have to know your audience! For the chili-head, try a dollop of sriracha. For the gourmet, a wee spoon of chicken liver or mushroom pâté, or even a single raw oyster. A cube of salty feta cheese with a ribbon of roasted red pepper is lovely, as are a few bits of cooked ham, bacon or smoked fish. Whatever you enjoy with an egg, put a bit of it at the bottom of the coddler.

Mother toted this precious egg coddler back home from Scotland in the late '70s. The loop on the lid sticks out from the simmering water for easy retrieval.

OMELETTE

Here's another one of those scarier-than-it-ought-to-be dishes. I watched a classic episode of Julia Child's *The French Chef*, in which she demonstrates the perfect French omelette. It was one of her later TV shows—it's in colour, she's rocking an orange blouse and wielding a non-stick pan. I'm not a fan of non-stick pans; unless you pay extra for the latest in non-toxic ceramic non-stick, the coatings can be hazardous to the health of you and your pets—especially birds.

Stick with 2- to 3-egg omelettes, any more than that will take too long to cook, and end up tough—the longer it takes to cook, says Julia, the tougher it will be. I can't argue with that. An omelette must be light, fluffy, pale and creamy.

There are those who add water—whisking in about ½ teaspoon (2.5 mL) per egg—and those who do not. Julia does; I don't, but I might start, since it was good enough for Julia!

For a 2- to 3-egg omelette, use a pan that measures 8 inches (20 cm) at the bottom. Julia has her pan over high heat, drops in about a tablespoon (15 mL) of butter and starts swirling it around, coating the bottom of the pan with sizzling butter. Now, she was cooking on an old 1970s electric stove, and I'm willing to bet her high heat was not quite as high as my blast furnace of a gas range, or perhaps yours, so bear that in mind.

When Julia or anyone else makes a classic French *omelette baveuse* (runny, dripping, creamy), there is no need for a spatula—you just add the eggs and swirl, tilt and jerk the pan toward you until they have formed a sort of loose log shape. And that's it.

The idea here is *not* a North American restaurant-perfect huge, spongy, browned and stuffed half-moon; it's all about the eggs. Butter, eggs, sea salt, freshly ground pepper, a garnish of finely chopped parsley, though I favour chives. *C'est tout, c'est complet!* If the eggs are not spectacularly fresh and truly free-run, there really is no point to something as simple as this, so in North America we load our omelettes up with all manner of distracting fillings and toppings.

Who's ready to give a classic French nude omelette a try?

POACHED

When I was a kid I watched Mother poach eggs in vinegared water—that's how she'd often eat them—but I failed to see the attraction; seemed like a lot of effort for something disappointing. Soggy toast. Vinegary egg. No butter. *No point!*

In my thirties I owned a restaurant, the Riverside Café, and that weekly hell called brunch forced me to find a new, better and faster way to poach eggs. I start by cracking an egg into a small dish. I put a shallow saucepan or small high-sided skillet full of water over medium-high heat, and bring it up to that perfect place between a simmer and a very gentle boil.

I slide the egg in, and just as soon as the whites begin to go opaque and look a little set, I gingerly slip a spatula under the egg to make sure it's not sticking to the pan. Once it's dislodged, it's safe to *gently* move it around a wee bit. If the water does not cover the yolk, use a spoon to baste the yolk with hot water to set it.

When the yolk is the preferred doneness—you'll be able to tell from looking, but 2 to 5 minutes should do it—use a slotted spoon to remove from the water since it's liable to slip off a flat spatula. I've never bothered draining eggs on a kitchen towel; I just rest the spoon on the counter with the egg sitting in it and let it drain onto a plate. No vinegar. No flyaway whites. No disappointment.

chinese marbled tea eggs

MAKES 6 EGGS

A Chinese New Year's treat, but pretty any time of year, I think. These are savoury and salty, just the way I like my hard-boiled eggs! As for the tea component: black tea is a very broad term and there are many types to be discovered. My friend Jennifer Commins is a tea importer and certified tea sommelier with her own company called Pluck Teas: I asked her what she would use for the best tea eggs. "A black tea such as English Breakfast would work, but a smoky tea like my Smoky Maple would be really interesting." Smoky Maple it is!

6 free-run eggs

¾ cup (180 mL) soy sauce

2 star anise pods

2 Tbsp (30 mL) looseleaf black tea

1 cinnamon stick

1 Tbsp (15 mL) maple syrup

1 Tbsp (15 mL) pink peppercorns

1 Tbsp (15 mL) black peppercorns

2 strips washed orange peel,
    about 3 inches (7.5 cm)

01. Add eggs to a medium saucepan and fill with enough cold water to cover the eggs with an extra inch (2.5 cm) over top. Set over high heat and bring to a gentle boil. As soon as the water has boiled, reduce heat to a simmer. Let simmer for about 3 minutes.

02. Lift the eggs out of the hot water—reserve the water and pot, we'll be using that!—and transfer the hot eggs to a colander in the sink. Run cold water over the eggs.

03. Once the eggs are cool enough to hold, take each one in your hand and with the back of a spoon, tap the shell to crack and dent it all over; the more cracks, the more colour and flavour will seep into the eggs. But keep in mind that you need to keep the shell holding together, so be judicious and as artsy-fartsy as you can!

04. Add the rest of the ingredients to the pot of hot water and give it a stir. Add the cracked eggs back in. Place over medium heat and bring back up to a gentle boil, then reduce heat to low and let simmer for about 15 minutes, covered. Turn heat off and leave the eggs to sit in the water overnight.

05. The next day, place the eggs back into the colander and rinse with cold water; set aside on a rack or kitchen towel to dry.

06. When completely dry, peel and reveal the prettiest eggs ever!

changua

SERVES 4

Oeufs en meurette is a classic French dish of eggs poached in red wine and served with a red wine and demi-glace enriched sauce. I find it too rich, but that doesn't mean you can't poach eggs in all sorts of other flavourful liquids; besides, you might like *oeufs en meurette!* Here are some others to try: broth, beer, cider, white wine, even milk. *Changua* is an incredibly rich and flavourful Colombian hangover helper of eggs poached in seasoned broth and milk. From what I've been able to learn about this jazzed-up version of milk toast, it's made by a doting parent or significant other for a loved one struck down by excess. When I shared this recipe with my Colombian friend Mary Luz, she was completely mystified. She'd not eaten it, heard of it or seen it on any menu. Clearly Mary Luz did not misspend her youth.

2 tsp (10 mL) butter or olive oil (or 1 tsp/5 mL) of each)

2 cloves garlic, finely minced

1½–2 cups (350–475 mL) diced potato

4 finely chopped scallions, divided

2 cups (475 mL) organic chicken broth

3 cups (710 mL) 3.5 percent milk (do not use skim milk or the soup will curdle)

Sea salt and freshly ground black pepper to taste

½ cup (120 mL) chopped fresh cilantro, plus more for garnish

4 free-run eggs

01. Into a large saucepan over medium heat, add the butter or oil, garlic, potatoes and about 3 of the chopped scallions; stir and cook for about 5 minutes.

02. Add the broth first, then the milk, and bring up to a very gentle boil. If you boil too aggressively, the soup will curdle.

03. Add salt, pepper and cilantro. Test one of the potato cubes; when they are almost tender, add the eggs to poach for about 3 minutes or until the yolks are done to your liking.

04. Sprinkle with more cilantro and the remaining chopped scallions and bring the pot to the table with a big ladle for dishing it up.

SIGNE LANGFORD PHOTO

Mary Luz and baby Natalie.

sweet lingonberry jam omelette

SERVES 2 FOR BREAKFAST OR DESSERT

The first dinner a boy ever cooked for me was an omelette; um . . . it was a night of other momentous firsts. I have a thing for omelettes. *Omelette soufflée à la confiture* is sweet and light, like our memories of youth.

And although "confiture" means jam or preserve, any sweet fruit spread or purée will work; I dare say Light and Fluffy Citrus Curd (page 111) would be brilliant.

¼ cup (60 mL) homemade or excellent-quality store-bought lingonberry jam, at room temperature
⅓ cup (80 mL) mascarpone, at room temperature
1 Tbsp (15 mL) freshly squeezed lemon juice
3 free-run eggs, separated
2 Tbsp (30 mL) super-fine vanilla sugar, divided
Pinch fine sea salt
2 Tbsp (30 mL) butter, divided
2 tsp (10 mL) icing sugar for garnish (optional)

01. In a medium bowl, add the jam, mascarpone and lemon juice and stir well to fully combine. Set aside.

02. Place egg yolks and 1 tablespoon (15 mL) of the vanilla sugar in a medium bowl and whisk until pale, creamy and beginning to thicken.

03. Place egg whites in a large bowl that has been wiped out with a drop of lemon juice and a clean kitchen towel. Add the remaining tablespoon (15 mL) sugar and a pinch of salt, and using electric beaters or a stand mixer with the whisk attachment, beat the whites until stiff peaks form.

04. Using a rubber spatula, gently fold the whites into the yolks until well combined, being careful not to collapse the whites.

05. Place a 10- to 12-inch (25- to 30- cm) skillet over medium heat. Add 1 tablespoon (15 mL) of the butter, melt and swirl around the skillet. Pour in the egg mixture and spread out to the edges, patting it down a bit. Cook for about 2 to 3 minutes, or until the eggs look just set. Do not let the omelette brown.

06. Using either an offset spatula or egg flipper, slide around the edges and underneath to make sure there are no stuck bits. When you're sure the omelette is loose, set a plate on top of the skillet and flip it over; the omelette should drop onto the plate. Wait a second and listen for the soft "plunk"!

07. Return the skillet to the heat and add the remaining butter; melt and swirl the butter, then slip the omelette back into the skillet. Continue to cook for about 2 to 3 minutes, or until the egg looks just set.

08. While the second side is cooking, spoon the jam-mascarpone filling over one half of the omelette. Tip the skillet, and with the help of a spatula, slip the omelette onto a serving platter, then fold the omelette in half. It won't be perfect—it shouldn't be perfect—the filling should be peeking out suggestively! Or, and this is my preferred way, skip this last stressful step and eat right out of the pan, tête-à-tête style.

09. Dust with icing sugar if you care to and serve immediately.

mother's pickled eggs

MAKES 12 EGGS

• •

Mother liked to pickle. It seemed out of character for this woman, an epitome of the seventies, all big hair, Librium, and dinner parties with Shirley Bassey, Burt Bacharach and Harry Belafonte LPs on the hi-fi. Still, when Father started piling cucumbers on the kitchen counter, she'd start pickling.

There was always a jar of pickled eggs on hand, and even after we no longer had our own hens, but rather received our weekly delivery of eggs from a woman who went door to door, her pet duck waddling behind her, *even then*, she'd order extra for pickling. Mother made them in the classic style, but she also played with beets and crabapples, tinting the whites pink. I can't say I ever noticed a book spread open on the counter; she seemed to do her pickling by memory or intuition.

I wasn't a fan of pickled eggs, and nor was Mother; Father was the one who'd wander in from the garden to dip his hand in the jar. They were a fixture of most homes in the country and in most taverns in town—a complimentary (and thirst-inducing) snack for every man who had bellied up to guzzle a Labatt's.

A while back, I was at a country farm-supply store, and there on the shelf were huge jars of pickled eggs. Such practical working-man's sustenance. What's not to love about that?

1 cup (250 mL) apple-cider vinegar
1 cup (250 mL) water
1 Tbsp (15 mL) sugar
2-inch (5-cm) knob fresh ginger root, peeled
    and very coarsely chopped
8 whole cloves
1 tsp (5 mL) allspice

1 tsp (5 mL) whole black or pink peppercorns
½ tsp (2.5 mL) mace
4-inch (10-cm) cinnamon stick
1 tsp (5 mL) sea salt
12 hard-boiled free-run eggs, peeled and rinsed
    (see Hard-Boiling: My Way, page 26)

01. Prepare canning jars and lids. I dip mine into a canning pot of boiling water and then dry, inverted, in a warm oven (350F/180C). Set aside.

02. Add vinegar, water, sugar, ginger and spices to a small saucepan over medium-high heat. Bring to a boil and stir until the sugar is dissolved; reduce to low heat, cover and simmer for about 10 minutes.

03. Add eggs to prepared jars. Here's your chance to add a few personalized things: a small stick of cinnamon, a star anise pod, a fresh bay leaf, a sprig of rosemary, some pink or other exotic peppercorns, cardamom pods, a crabapple or two, or baby beets. Be you, experiment!

04. Now pour the hot pickling liquid into the jars almost to the top, distributing the cooked spices and ginger bits between the jars.

05. Screw the lids on tight. Let the jars cool before popping them into the refrigerator, and don't taste them yet! They'll taste of nothing; they need at least 2 to 3 days to soak up some flavour, and they're at their best after 2 weeks. Keep refrigerated; will last in the refrigerator for up to 3 months.

my devilled eggs

Here's a dish that lends itself to many flavours—curry, Tex-Mex, Provençal, Asian—but for me, the classic, the one that started it all, is just about perfect. And seriously dangerous! Have you ever noticed that while you might never even consider eating four eggs for breakfast, that many *and more* easily slide down the gullet once devilled? Well, perhaps not my late mother's rather dry and bland specimens, but those little devils that strike just the right note of creamy, fatty, savoury goodness go down like greased lightning.

Mother didn't get all fancy and pipe the yolks back into the whites; she'd just push a little mound off a teaspoon with her pinky finger, then finish with a shake of paprika. She only ever used her pinky, saying there were no germs on that finger. I'm not worried about germs, but I do think it really looks great if you can pipe. They look even better on one of those vintage devilled egg plates that turn up all the time in thrift and second-hand shops, and there are lots of new ones in shops now too; they're coming back into vogue.

5 hard-boiled free-run eggs, peeled and rinsed
   (see Hard-Boiling: My Way, page 26)
¼ tsp (1 mL) fine sea salt, or more to taste
¼ tsp (1 mL) white pepper, or more to taste
1 tsp (5 mL) dry mustard
¼ cup (60 mL) mayonnaise
1 tsp (5 mL) pickle juice
Paprika for garnish

01. Slice the eggs in half lengthwise. Dipping a sharp knife in hot water and cleaning off on a damp dishrag between eggs is a good way to keep the final look clean and fresh. Pop out the yolks and add them to a small bowl; you can pass them through a ricer too, if you like them extra fluffy.

02. Arrange the whites on a specialized plate or on top of a lettuce leaf–lined plate; otherwise they will slide all around.

03. Add the remaining ingredients and stir until super well-blended and smooth, or blend in a food processor. Once totally smooth and blended, add the yolk mixture back into the egg whites using either a piping bag or a spoon (with your pinky, natch!).

04. Finish with a pinch or sprinkle of paprika, plain or smoked.

---

devilled green goddess eggs and ham:
Add 1 very ripe avocado and some very finely chopped ham or prosciutto to the mix and you've got, well, you know . . .

devilled bacon and eggs: Add finely diced crispy fried bacon to the mix.

herbed devilled eggs: Add chopped capers to the mix, then top with a generous sprinkling of finely chopped fresh chives.

Fresh snipped herb sprouts make pretty garnishes for devilled eggs.

garnishes for devilled eggs

CAVIAR: I like Canadian farmed caviar and even the new vegan stuff made with a combination of seaweed and science.

FINELY CHOPPED FRESH HERBS: Anything you like really—but chives, parsley, tarragon, chervil, fennel frond, cilantro, dill and basil are tops.

FRIED HERBS AND CAPERS: Whole fried herb leaves—basil or sage— or crispy fried capers. Drain the capers well in a sieve, then blot using kitchen towel: pat down and really dry them well. Add to hot oil and watch them blossom! Lift out with slotted spoon and drain on a kitchen towel.

ONION: Finely minced shallot and green or purple onion add a nice crunch and some bite.

PICKLES: A dash of dill pickle, pickled hot peppers, capers, olives, pickled green beans. A smidgeon of pickled beet with its juice bleeding over the yolk is kind of gorgeous.

SMOKED OR SALTED FISH: A tiny bit of smoked salmon, trout, mackerel or butterfish is really luscious. A fleck of anchovy adds a nice salty backbone.

TOASTED SESAME SEEDS: Black or white add a hit of toastiness. Also, look for the Japanese seasoning blend that contains sesame and seaweed specks; it's an umami blast.

WASABI: Either a sprinkling of the powdered kind or a dab of the paste.

meeru's curried devilled eggs

MAKES 12 DEVILLED EGGS PLUS EXTRA FILLING FOR SANDWICHES OR SNACKING

Here's a very special recipe from *Vij's at Home: Relax, Honey* by Meeru Dhalwala and Vikram Vij. Vij writes:

"This recipe was inspired by a feast of boiled eggs with various Ukrainian condiments and white wine at the home of our friends Oleg and Victoria. After that meal, Meeru started eating boiled eggs with Ukrainian horseradish for breakfast. It was a healthy, quick meal that filled her up for a few hours. When she ate one of these eggs at a managers' meeting one morning, however, the staff complained that the smell interfered with the aroma of their coffee. So we don't recommend these curried eggs for breakfast, but they're great as hors d'oeuvres with a glass of white wine or bubbly."

¼ cup (60 mL) cooking oil

½ tsp (2.5 mL) whole cumin seeds

1 cup (250 mL) chopped red onion

1 Tbsp (15 mL) finely chopped garlic

½ cup (120 mL) finely chopped tomato

½ tsp (2.5 mL) fine sea salt

1 tsp (5 mL) crushed cayenne pepper (optional)

½ tsp (2.5 mL) ground cumin or garam masala

½ tsp (2.5 mL) ground fenugreek seeds (optional)

Dash freshly ground black pepper

¼ cup (60 mL) plain yogurt (minimum 2 percent milkfat), stirred

6 free-run eggs, hard-boiled, cooled to room temperature and peeled (see Hard-Boiling: My Way, page 26)

Quarter of a large jalapeno pepper, seeded and finely chopped, for garnish

01. Heat oil in a small saucepan over medium-high heat for about 1 minute. Add cumin seeds and allow them to sizzle for 30 seconds, or until the seeds are dark brown but not black. Add onion and sauté for 4 minutes, or until light golden. Add garlic and sauté for another 2 to 3 minutes, or until golden brown.

02. Stir in tomato, then immediately add salt, cayenne (if using), ground cumin or garam masala, fenugreek seeds (if using) and black pepper. Sauté the masala for 4 to 5 minutes or until oil glistens on top. Remove from heat.

03. Place yogurt in a small bowl. To prevent curdling, spoon 1 tablespoon (15 mL) of the hot masala into the yogurt. Stir well, then pour the yogurt into the masala. Place over medium heat and mix well but gently. Cook for 3 minutes, stirring continuously, then remove from the heat.

04. Cut eggs in half lengthwise and carefully scoop the yolks into a medium bowl. Place whites on a devilled egg tray or lettuce-lined plate so they don't slide around. Mash yolks with a fork until they are smooth (don't add any water).

05. Add the warm masala sauce to yolks and mix well. Using a teaspoon, stuff egg white halves with the filling. Sprinkle a pinch of the jalapeno pepper over each egg half.

06. Serve immediately or cover and refrigerate for about 30 minutes, or until chilled.

creamy shirred eggs with melted gouda

SERVES 4

Those of us on this side of The Pond don't do this enough: bake eggs in heavy cream. I resolve to shirr more eggs! Basically, it's an individual oven-proof dish, buttered, with an egg or two cracked in and a drizzle of heavy cream. Sometimes cheese, ham or other tasty things are added. This method is different from coddling in a few ways: it's cooked uncovered and exposed to dry heat, and unlike coddling (which is done in a cup-like, lidded vessel), shirring should be done in a wider and shallower oven-proof dish.

2 Tbsp (30 mL) softened butter, for buttering the dishes
8 free-run eggs
Sea salt and freshly ground black pepper to taste
½ cup (120 mL) 35 percent cream
½ cup (120 mL) grated gouda (I like Thunder Oak gouda from Ontario)
1 Tbsp (15 mL) finely chopped fresh flat-leaf parsley (leaves only)
1 Tbsp (15 mL) finely chopped fresh chives

01. Preheat oven to 375F (190C). Butter 4 individual ramekins or other oven-proof dishes, approximately 6-ounce (175-mL) capacity. Set ramekins on baking sheet.

02. Add 2 eggs into each buttered dish and season with salt and pepper.

03. Pop the eggs in the oven to bake on their own for about 5 minutes, then remove and top each dish with about 2 tablespoons (30 mL) cream, 2 tablespoons (30 mL) cheese and the fresh herbs.

04. Return to the oven and continue to bake for a further 10 to 15 minutes, or until bubbly and set up. Serve immediately with buttered toast.

THAT AIN'T CHICKEN FEED!

my kinda perfect egg salad sandwiches

MAKES 2 WELL-STUFFED SANDWICHES

One of life's simplest and purest pleasures is a really well-made sandwich, am I right? When the bread is super-fresh and absolutely right for the job, the filling perfect in taste and texture, and the ratio of main event, vehicle and garnishes stacked in perfect proportions, well, that is a *real joy*. A decent dill, a handful of salty kettle-cooked chips on the plate, a pint of cider, and I'm in lunchtime heaven.

For the perfect egg salad sandwich, at least for me, it has to be soft, squishy white bread with thin crusts, or no crusts at all, like those English tea dainties. The filling should be creamy, savoury, rich and tangy, punctuated with the crunch of diced pickle, the occasional surprise of coarsely ground fresh black pepper, and the herbal freshness of chives, parsley or even tarragon, should you be feeling *très* French that day.

I've suggested using medium-hard boiled eggs, simply because the yolk will be creamier and a deeper, more vibrant yellow, but all the way hard-boiled is perfectly fine if that's what you prefer.

4 free-run medium-hard or hard-boiled eggs
    (see Hard-Boiling: My Way, page 26)
2 Tbsp (30 mL) Sunshine-Yellow Homemade
    Mayonnaise, recipe on page 48 (or good quality
    free-run store-bought)
¼ tsp (1 mL) Worcestershire sauce
½ tsp (2.5 mL) garlic powder
½ tsp (2.5 mL) onion powder
2 Tbsp (30 mL) finely diced crunchy dill pickle
½ tsp (2.5 mL) pickle juice

2 Tbsp (30 mL) finely chopped fresh chive
Pinch sea salt, or more to taste
Freshly ground black pepper to taste
4 slices good-quality, thin-crusted, soft white
    sandwich bread
Softened butter for spreading
4 leaves iceberg lettuce

01. Slice the eggs by hand or with an egg slicer and add to a large bowl; it's a good head start and it eliminates chasing slippery eggs around the bowl.

02. Add the rest of the filling ingredients and mash with a fork, potato masher or even a pastry cutter, leaving some larger chunks of egg. Switch to a spatula for the final blending. Taste and adjust for salt and pepper.

03. Generously butter the bread on both sides; don't skip this step or you will end up with soggy bread. Add lettuce to one side, top with egg mixture and spread almost to the edges. None of this scoop-of-egg-in-the-middle, empty bread all around the edges nonsense.

classic hollandaise sauce

MAKES ABOUT 1½ CUPS (350 ML)

Hollandaise is another one of those culinary words that strike fear into the hearts of cooks and non-cooks alike, and there's just no reason for it. Don't tell anyone I said this, but making a decent Hollandaise is one of those things that fancy chefs want us to think is super-difficult and not to be attempted by mere culinary mortals, lest the delicate sauce "break" and the world as we know end on a Sunday, right before brunch, with everyone still hungry and quite possibly hungover.

True, it does break—curdle, separate—from time to time, but there's a cheat for that, called mousse-line. I worked many a busy brunch shift and, believe you me, when there were a million chits waggling in my sweaty face and the Hollandaise curdled,

the first thing to go would be my terrified kitchen staff—they'd tiptoe to the hall and watch from a safe distance, knowing that the next thing to go would be my cool. But, I learned right quick that a broken Hollandaise can be mended very nicely by adding a drop of cold cream, whisking like mad, and never speaking of it again. Like magic, the Hollandaise would become one again, a stiff drink would appear on the counter behind me, brunch would carry on and the world would keep spinning on its slightly wobbly axis.

So, here's a classic Hollandaise—one of the five mother sauces of classical French cuisine—once you've mastered this, believe me, you will feel like a superstar!

SIGNE LANGFORD PHOTO

4 free-run egg yolks

1 Tbsp (15 mL) freshly squeezed lemon juice

½ tsp (2.5 mL) sea salt

Pinch ground white pepper

Pinch cayenne powder

½ cup (120 mL) room temperature butter,
    cut into small chunks

01. Set a double boiler or bain-marie over medium heat, so that the water is simmering well (see the How to Make a Bain-Marie sidebar).

02. Into the top of the double boiler or bain-marie, add the yolks, lemon juice, salt, pepper and cayenne. And start whisking. Remember to keep checking the heat of the water—take a look, reduce heat if it's boiling—and feel the sides of the double boiler or bowl; if it's allowed to overheat you'll have scrambled yolks.

03. Now, while whisking continuously, start adding the butter about 1 tablespoon (15 mL) at a time. Only add the next knob of butter once the preceding one has been fully incorporated into the yolks.

04. Remember to keep the heat down and the sauce moving to prevent breaking or scrambling. Once the last bit of butter has been added and incorporated, taste for seasoning and adjust to suit your tastes.

05. Serve immediately over a perfectly poached egg (see page 31) or tender asparagus. Reheating Hollandaise is a bit tricky—it *can* be done, but it's fussy and usually requires the addition of a bit of water or heavy cream. So, eat up!

how to make a bain-marie or jerry-rig a double boiler

Even if you own a proper double boiler, sometimes what you really need is a makeshift one, because I find the size and shape of the top pot is often too small and too narrow: not conducive to expansive whisking. So if you've never done this before, here's an illustration of how to set it up.

You don't need a dedicated double boiler; do what most chefs do and rig up a bain-marie. I prefer it; the bowl is a better shape for whisking curds and custards.

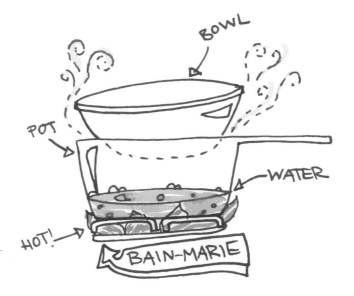

sunshine-yellow homemade mayonnaise

MAKES 1 CUP (250 ML)

My German ex-mother-in-law was many things, some I'd prefer to forget—you try spiriting a 19-year-old blond-haired, blue-eyed boy away from a confirmed hausfrau and see what happens! But, to her credit, the woman opened my eyes to a few culinary wonders: cold German fruit soup (a revelation), gorgeous German wines (also a revelation to a 17-year-old small-town girl) and homemade mayonnaise. Mother bought No Name mayo, so to see this magical thing happen in her stand mixer and then taste its eggy wondrousness over a warm German baby potato salad was . . . you guessed it . . . a revelation. As you experiment with homemade mayonnaise, play with what mustard you use; flavoured mustards add a nice element of surprise.

2 free-run egg yolks
1 tsp (5 mL) smooth Dijon mustard
5 tsp (25 mL) freshly squeezed lemon juice
1 cup (250 mL) vegetable or olive oil, or a mix
    of your favourite oils
¼ tsp (1 mL) sea salt
¼ tsp (1 mL) white pepper

01. Add yolks to the bowl of a stand mixer with a whisk attachment (or food processor) and begin whisking on high speed.
02. Add mustard and lemon juice and continue to whisk or blend until well combined.
03. Now, this is the magical bit; as the beater is going, very slowly drizzle in the oil in a very thin stream. In a little time, and if the mayonnaise gods are with you, it will emulsify into creamy, dreamy stuff. Don't expect the same lily-white fluffy stuff you buy in a jar, this mayo is more yellow and can be much less voluminous. Stop once or twice to scrape down the sides of the bowl.
04. Add the salt and pepper and blend it in.
05. Transfer to a container and store, covered, for up to 3 days in the fridge.

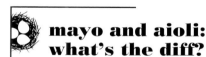

mayo and aioli: what's the diff?

In a word: garlic. Garlic—well, okay, maybe a few other subtleties—is the difference between good old homemade mayo and Mediterranean aioli. In fact, many restaurant menus play fast and loose with the word "aioli" by simply adding a splash more lemon juice and some garlic to commercial mayo. Some aioli purists insist on making it with a mortar and pestle, and the yolk-oil ratio is a tad different . . . but you get the idea.

classic caesar

SERVES 2 FOR LUNCH OR 4 AS A SIDE

When it was created by restaurateur and hotelier Caesar Cardini around about 1930, this salad was always prepared tableside. Good luck finding that sort of showmanship in a dining room today, but when I was in my twenties, there was one rare old-school bastion of the Caesar in Montreal. An elderly man would come shuffling out of the kitchen pushing a trolley loaded up with a giant wooden bowl, his *mise en place*, a bar towel draped over one arm. First, he'd rub the bottom of the bowl with a cut clove of garlic. Then he'd grate fresh cheese followed by a grind of pepper, anchovy and yolk of a fresh egg he'd crack and separate. A quick wipe of his hands on his fresh white towel, followed by a squeeze of lemon, and with that he'd whip it into a perfect emulsion with a fork. Romaine and croutons—no bacon—were tossed, the salad served and he'd shuffle back though the flapping kitchen doors.

⅓ cup (80 mL) diced guanciale or bacon (optional)
1 clove garlic, cut in half
3 anchovies
Freshly ground black pepper to taste
1 free-run egg yolk
Juice of 1 lemon
Dash of Tabasco
Dash of Worcestershire sauce
Pinch dry mustard
⅓ cup (80 mL) freshly grated pecorino
¼ cup (60 mL) extra-virgin olive oil
1 head romaine lettuce, outer leaves removed,
    inner leaves washed and well dried
1 cup (250 mL) croutons

01. If using, add guanciale or bacon to a skillet and cook over medium-high heat until crispy; transfer with slotted spoon to a clean kitchen towel and set aside. The rendered fat is good for roasted potatoes, so don't toss that.

02. Rub a large wooden salad bowl with the cut ends of the garlic. Depending on the texture of the bowl, it might actually act as a grater and pulverize the garlic; that would be very handy! If not, use a Microplane or garlic press to extract the garlic oil.

03. Add the anchovies and pepper and blend with the garlic. A wooden salad server (spoon) works well for this, as the anchovies will need some smooshing against the side of the bowl.

04. Add the egg yolk, lemon juice, Tabasco, Worcestershire, mustard and about 2 table-spoons (30 mL) of the cheese. Whisk continuously as you add the oil in a thin, slow stream.

05. Add the guanciale, lettuce, croutons and remaining cheese to the bowl, and toss well to evenly coat. Add an extra grind or so of pepper if you like.

SIGNE LANGFORD PHOTO

cinnamon-vanilla baked custard

SERVES 6

This custard is more like a pudding, and it's not nearly as rich as Crème Anglaise (page 51); more of an any-day dessert.

3 cups (710 mL) 3.5 percent milk
4 free-run eggs
½ cup (120 mL) sugar
1½ tsp (7.5 mL) pure vanilla extract
¼ tsp (1 mL) sea salt
Pinch freshly grated nutmeg
Pinch ground cinnamon or more to taste

01. Preheat oven to 350F (180C). Butter six 6-ounce (¾-cup/175-mL) ramekins, or other oven-safe vessels. Set the buttered dishes into a roasting pan and fill the pan with hot water up to the halfway mark on the dishes.

02. In a medium saucepan over medium heat, heat milk up until it's very hot, but not boiling. When hot, remove from heat.

03. While the milk is heating, in a large bowl, whisk together the eggs, sugar, vanilla and salt. Whisk until well blended, but don't make it frothy.

04. When the milk is hot, very gradually add to the egg mixture in a very thin stream, while whisking briskly.

05. Transfer the mixture to a jug, or use a ladle to equally fill the ramekins with the liquid custard. Sprinkle the tops with nutmeg and cinnamon to taste.

06. Pop into the oven and bake for about 25 to 30 minutes, or until a knife inserted into the custard comes out clean. Keep in mind the custard is still going to be quite soft at this point; it will solidify as it cools.

07. Take the ramekins from the water bath and either serve them right away or set them out on a rack to cool, uncovered. Once cool, cover and keep in the fridge for up to 3 days.

FEATHERS ARE GOING TO FLY!

crème anglaise

MAKES ABOUT 1 CUP (250 ML)

Yes, you can buy something sort of like this in tins now, but homemade is super-easy, the flavour is amazing and there's really nothing quite like the aromas of cream and vanilla floating around the kitchen.

½ cup (120 mL) 3.5 percent milk
½ cup (120 mL) 35 percent cream
Half a vanilla bean, split lengthwise,
    seeds scraped out
3 free-run egg yolks
3 Tbsp (45 mL) sugar

01. In a heavy-bottomed medium saucepan over medium heat, add the milk, cream and scraped-out seeds from the vanilla-bean half. Bring to a simmer, then remove from heat; set aside.
02. In a medium bowl, whisk egg yolks and sugar to fully blend.
03. Ever so gradually, whisk the hot milk into the yolks in a thin stream; keep whisking so as not to scramble the yolks. Return to the saucepan and place over low heat. Do not allow to boil.
04. Stir constantly until thickened. It'll be done when it coats the back of a spoon and your finger leaves a path when dragged through, 5 minutes or so.
05. Set a sieve over a jug or container and strain the custard through for any icky little bits of cooked egg. Cool to room temperature uncovered, then cover and chill in the fridge. You can make this a day ahead if need be.
06. Serve drizzled over plain cakes, fresh fruit or chocolate ice cream.

vanilla-bean bonanza

Often a recipe will call for half a vanilla bean or pod, or ask you to simply split and scrape but not use the actual pod. Yes, you can put that half bean away for another day, but what about the scraped pod? Well, it's still got a lot of life left in it—don't chuck it! You can add it to a bag or jar of sugar for lovely vanilla sugar, pop it into a mickey of vodka or Canadian rye for a real treat, or cut it up to toss it into your ladies' nesting boxes. What girl doesn't like a sweet-smelling boudoir?

lemon heaven

This divine discovery was the result of an act of late-night desperation. I wanted something sweet (I may have been feeling sorry for myself; ice-cream-level sorry for myself) but naturally I didn't have any ice cream. But I did find two mason jars in the fridge, one full of citrus curd (recipe on page 111) and one full of Crème Anglaise. So naturally, I dumped them together into the ice-cream maker and cranked my way to heaven. Sweet, sweet lemony heaven.

tip

Covering and cooling a warm curd or custard in the fridge creates condensation that drips back down onto the surface, leaving puddles, pale spots and pockmarks!

luscious all-purpose pastry cream

MAKES ABOUT 1½ CUPS (350 ML)

. . . .

This is a lightly vanilla-scented pastry cream that employs a bit of cornstarch for stability and structure.

2 Tbsp (30 mL) butter, cut or pulled into small bits
3 free-run egg yolks
3 Tbsp (45 mL) sugar
2 Tbsp (30 mL) cornstarch
1 cup (250 mL) 3.5 percent milk
Half a vanilla bean, split lengthwise,
    seeds scraped out

01. Add the butter bits to a large bowl with a strainer set over it and set aside. In a large bowl, whisk the egg yolks, sugar and cornstarch; set aside.

02. Into a medium saucepan over medium-low heat, add the milk and scraped vanilla seeds; bring up to just nearly simmering.

03. Gradually whisk the hot milk into the egg mixture in a very thin, slow stream, whisking like crazy to prevent scrambling! Once it's all in the bowl and whisked, return it all to the pot and place back over medium-low heat, whisking constantly. You'll need to use a silicon spatula every now and then to scrape down the sides so it doesn't cook dry and hard.

04. Whisk and cook until nicely thickened and glossy, about 2 to 4 minutes. Pour through the strainer over the butter—help it pass through the strainer with your whisk or spatula if needed—then whisk the butter in.

05. Transfer to a bowl and allow to come to room temperature. Cover, then chill in the fridge until you're ready to make something divine with it. But use it up within about 4 days.

Combined with a simple choux pastry base (page 54), this versatile cream is what makes cream puffs, éclairs and *mille-feuille* so luscious.

blank slate choux pastry

MAKES ABOUT 30 ÉCLAIR OR CREAM PUFF SHELLS

Called *pâte* à *choux* in French, this is a most delicious starting point for so many classic pastries, including my beloved *mille-feuille*. Here's a perfect, blank-slate recipe from master baker Bonnie Gordon.

1½ cups (355 mL) water

4 tsp (20 mL) sugar

1 tsp (5 mL) fine sea salt

6 oz (170 g) / ¾ cup (180 mL) butter, room temperature, cut into small pieces

7.4 oz (210 g) / 1½ cups (350 mL) bread flour, sifted

1 free-run egg white

Up to 6 free-run eggs

01. Preheat oven to 425F (220C) and line a baking sheet with parchment paper.

02. In a large saucepan over medium heat, combine water, sugar, salt and butter and bring to a simmer. Do not boil!

03. Add the flour, blend with a wooden spoon and continue to cook and stir over medium heat for about 2 minutes, or until the dough comes together into a silky, smooth ball.

04. Transfer the dough to the bowl of a stand mixer, or large bowl, and allow to cool for about 5 minutes. Using the paddle attachment or a wooden spoon, add the egg white and then the eggs one at a time, stirring to fully incorporate each egg before adding the next. Continue to add eggs one at a time until the dough is liquid enough to pipe but stiff enough to hold its shape on the tray. You may not use all 6 eggs in the end.

05. Pipe into desired shape onto a parchment-lined baking sheet: balls for profiteroles and bars for éclairs. Keep in mind, this dough will expand quite a bit, so give a good 3 inches (7.5 cm) between each.

06. Bake until starting to brown, then turn the heat down to 375F (190C) and continue baking until golden brown. Transfer to a wire rack to cool completely before using.

OPPOSITE, CLOCKWISE FROM TOP: Miss Vicky taking care of business! (DG); a selection of heritage eggs from the girls on Murray's Farm (SL); the aftermath of Miss Vicky's wing trimming (DG).

sweet italian zabaglione

MAKES 1 CUP (250 ML)

I knew I was in the presence of worldly folks—so much more worldly than I—when after dinner at my neighbours' apartment, Howard, a Ph.D. student, started clearing the table while his wife, Ellen, a translator, began whipping up a batch of boozy, frothy, unbelievably rich and super-quick zabaglione. I'd never tasted it before, let alone seen it made, and what struck me was the astonishing simplicity of it. I think we North Americans either over-complicate or over-process the foods we eat. This was simply eggs, sugar, fortified wine, a little heat and some elbow grease *et voilà!*

Marsala is the classic, but these spirits will work too: Vin Santo, amaretto, sweet sherry, almost anything really, but you'll have to take into account the sweetness of the spirit and adjust the sugar you add to the yolks.

¼ cup (60 mL) Marsala, Vin Santo or nutty liqueur
4 tsp (20 mL) super-fine (berry) sugar
4 free-run egg yolks

01. Set up a double boiler or bain-marie (see sidebar on page 47) and add the spirit, sugar and yolks; whisk briskly until it thickens to a custard-like consistency, about 6 minutes.

02. Be very mindful of the temperature and take the mixture off the heat as needed to keep it from cooking and scrambling. If you're nervous, set up a bowl of ice water nearby to dunk the bottom of the pot or bowl into for a rapid cool-down.

03. Zabaglione is meant to be enjoyed within 5 minutes of coming off the heat! To serve, simply spoon while warm into delicate little dessert dishes, wine glasses or ice-cream dishes. Or serve with fresh fruit, toasted sliced almonds, or a slice of plain pound or angel food cake.

savoury french sabayon

MAKES 1 CUP (250 ML)

In Italy it's zabaglione. In France, sabayon, and in French cuisine, a sabayon can be sweet or savoury. The savoury version is traditionally made with champagne and used to dress delicate white fish or shellfish. When picking the bubbles, don't go for the driest you can find—a touch of residual sugar will serve this dish well.

¼ cup (60 mL) dry champagne
¼ cup (60 mL) 35 percent cream
Pinch sea salt
Pinch white pepper
1 tsp (5 mL) very finely minced fresh chives, parsley, tarragon, thyme or cilantro
4 free-run egg yolks

01. Set up a double boiler or bain-marie (see sidebar on page 47) and add the champagne, cream, salt, pepper, herbs and yolks; whisk briskly until it thickens to a custard-like consistency, about 6 minutes.

02. Be very mindful of the temperature and take the mixture off the heat as needed to keep it from cooking and scrambling. If you're nervous, set up a bowl of ice water nearby to dunk the bottom of the bowl into for a rapid cool-down. And that's it! Once nice and thick, serve with delicately flavoured fish, shellfish, poached chicken, boiled potatoes, green beans or asparagus.

SIGNE LANGFORD PHOTO

ancient salt-cured yolks

Sounds weird, I know, but I think there's a certain romance to some of these old-time recipes that were born purely of necessity. If refrigeration had always been available, we might not have cured and smoked foods, and what a shame that would be.

Preserving yolks in a deep bed of salt renders them very firm (reminiscent of a hard cheese such as Parmesan), preserves their bright-orange colour and transforms them into a rich condiment for grating over pastas, salads or potato dishes. This adds richness and much interest when brought out to the table with a Microplane on the side.

Kosher or coarse sea salt
Granulated sugar (optional)
As many free-run egg yolks as you want
    to preserve

01. Take a non-reactive container—a glass casserole dish is good for this—and cover the bottom of the dish with a deep layer (about 3 inches/7.5 cm) of your preferred salt mixture. You can use only salt, or a 60:40 sugar to salt blend. Get a little creative and use a bit of truffle salt, chili- or herb-infused salt, or even a smoked salt. Or how about vanilla sugar?

02. Use the back of a teaspoon to make little depressions for the yolks to sit in. Separate as many eggs as you want to cure, placing each yolk in its own dish, then very gingerly tip the yolks out of their dishes and into the indents in the salt. Cover with another deep layer of your salt mixture and place them in the fridge, uncovered, for about 7 days.

03. For each yolk, prepare a double-layered 6-inch (15-cm) square of cheesecloth and a 12-inch (30-cm) length of kitchen twine. You'll also need to figure out a method for suspending the yolks in the fridge—I use a wire egg basket, natch!

04. After 7 days, you'll need to dig the yolks out, and here you'll want to be as careful as an archeologist digging up dino bones; the yolks are still fragile. Gently brush off the excess salt using a pastry brush, then set each yolk into the centre of a cheesecloth square. Pull the corners of the cheesecloth up around each yolk like a little coin purse, and cinch shut with a length of kitchen twine. Suspend the bundles in the fridge and there they will stay for about 3 more weeks, until they are almost rock-hard. Wrapped in cheesecloth and suspended for air circulation, the preserved yolks will keep for several months in the fridge.

so you've made hollandaise sauce—
what do you do with all those egg whites?

An egg white (sometimes referred to as albumen) is mostly water and protein. That's why those high-maintenance fitness types order egg-white omelettes at brunch (wilted spinach, whole-grain toast, no butter, no-fat latte, no fun)—because there's almost zero fat in the white. As far as I'm concerned, the yolk—a rich, runny one—is the best part of the egg, but whites are so very useful in the kitchen. They leaven cakes, bind batters, froth cocktails and even clarify broths. Egg whites turn up in pharmaceuticals, art supplies, cosmetics and so much more, but we're just going to make some incredibly tasty goodies with them.

CRYSTAL-CLEAR CONSOMMÉ

Whisk up a couple of egg whites to add to a murky broth, and watch as the egg-white "raft" slurps up all the impurities. Simply bring to a very low simmer for about 15 minutes, then strain it all through cheesecloth. Give that egg white to your backyard girls!

EGG WHITES FOR CRISPY FRIES

Not only do frothed-up egg whites make great food "glue," they also help achieve crispiness with difficult ingredients, such as sweet potatoes. I really wanted to hop on the sweet-potato fries bandwagon but could not get it right at home, time after time coming up with limp sweet potato sticks when I wanted healthy and crispy oven fries.

Egg whites turned out to be the answer. If you've not tried this yet, the ratio is one frothed-up egg white to two peeled and julienned sweet potatoes.

Whisk an egg white in a medium bowl with salt, pepper, ½ tsp (2.5 mL) cornstarch and whatever spices you like. Add in the cut potato and toss to coat well and evenly. Tumble onto a lightly oiled or parchment-lined cookie sheet and bake at 425F (220C) for about 40 to 45 minutes or until golden in spots.

RISE UP!

Whisking egg whites pumps them full of air. Take a really close look at a bowl of egg whites as you begin whisking; first you'll see some big bubbles, then they'll become smaller and more numerous as you whisk. When whipped egg whites are carefully folded into cake or other batters, then baked in the oven, the air trapped inside each and every tiny bubble expands, making the bubbles bigger and causing the whole mixture to rise.

tip

Egg whites, yolks and whole eggs freeze beautifully. I wouldn't use a once-frozen egg for poaching and eating on toast, but for baking they're perfectly fine.

maple-chipotle ontario pecans

MAKES 2 CUPS (475 ML)

In this recipe, egg whites act as glue, binding the sugar and spice and everything nice to the nuts. My favourite nut of all time is the pecan. It goes into my numero-uno pie and harmonizes beautifully with my all-time favourite flavour—maple. I realize some folks are going to be outraged by this last predilection—I'm looking at you, Maple-Walnut People—but I stand by my fetish. Pecans are soft but crisp, sweet and never bitter, the way a walnut can be sometimes. I demand predictability from my nuts! And now that I've learned that Canada (Ontario and British Columbia in particular) has a burgeoning nut-growing industry to support, I'm on a mission: eat more local pecans! Still, if you really don't like pecans, go ahead and use any nut you prefer—I won't hold it against you.

These are smoky, sweet, crunchy and maple-y; all of my favourite things!

1 free-run egg white
1 tsp (5 mL) water
Pinch fine sea salt
8 oz (225 g) raw Ontario pecans
    (about 2 cups/475 mL)
⅓ cup (80 mL) maple sugar or maple flakes
1–2 tsp (5–10 mL) chipotle powder
1 tsp (5 mL) chunky sea salt or kosher salt

01. Preheat oven to 300F (150C) and line a large baking sheet with parchment paper.
02. In a large bowl, whisk the egg white, water and fine salt until slightly frothy.
03. Add the pecans to the egg whites and stir well to coat. Set a sieve over another bowl and dump the eggy nuts into the sieve to drain off any excess white. Let drain for a couple of minutes, giving it a couple of shakes while it drains. (Cooked egg-white clumps on the finished nuts are not delightful!)
04. While the nuts are draining, add the maple sugar, chipotle powder and coarse salt to another large bowl and stir to blend. Add the drained nuts, stir and toss to evenly coat.
05. Tumble the coated nuts onto the prepared baking sheet—spread them out into a single layer—and bake for 40 to 45 minutes, rotating the sheet once during baking time.
06. Once cooled, the nuts will have stuck together in places; just break them apart before serving or storing in an airtight container.

raspberry-rose gin flip

MAKES 2 COCKTAILS

When lavender was in everything from steak rubs to shortbread cookies, I was against it. It was just too reminiscent of one of those sachets old ladies used to keep in their undies drawer. But rose, now that's another story. I love it! In bath bubbles, perfume, desserts and cocktails—especially gin cocktails since rose is one of the aromatics used in my favourite gin, Hendrick's. Doesn't hurt that it's a Scottish gin. I also love a cocktail made with an egg white; it's creamy, frothy and smooth. And when they're fresh backyard eggs it's even better.

1 oz (30 mL) gin
2 Tbsp (30 mL) rose syrup (see sidebar)
1 Tbsp (15 mL) homemade raspberry jam (or
    substitute excellent-quality store-bought)
1 free-run egg white

01. Add all ingredients to a cocktail shaker with ice. Shake vigorously and pour into 2 pretty glasses; hold back the ice cubes, but don't strain. Garnish with rose petals if you can find some organic ones!

 ## rose syrup

To make rose syrup, add **⅓ cup (80 mL) rosewater** and **3 tablespoons (45 mL) vanilla sugar** to a small saucepan and bring up to a simmer. Cook, stirring often, for about 5 minutes. Set aside and allow to cool. Make it the day before so it's really cold.

ontario pecan-maple coconut macaroons

MAKES ABOUT 2 DOZEN COOKIES

Don't you just hate it when you find the cookie to beat all other cookies and the bakery just stops making them? No warning. They're just not there anymore.

Arz Bakery in North York, Ontario, is where I fell in love with the best coconut macaroon I've ever tasted. Ever. In my entire life. It was big: about four inches across its golden crunchiness. And oh, so golden and crunchy on the outside and gooey chewy on the inside. It was sweet, with edges that were extra crisp, and the sort of cookie that requires important decisions be made: tough choices like deciding whether the last bite will be a crunchy edge bit or the sweet and soft centre. And then it was gone . . .

But take heart: here's a recipe I came up with to take the sting out of this situation and I think they're even better! So there!

4 free-run egg whites
½ cup (120 mL) granulated sugar
Pinch fine sea salt
1½ tsp (7.5 mL) maple extract
4¼ cups (1 L) sweetened shredded coconut
½ cup (120 mL) coarsely chopped raw pecans

01. Preheat oven to 325F (160C) and line 2 baking sheets with parchment.
02. In the bowl of a stand mixer or in a large bowl with an electric mixer, beat the egg whites, sugar, salt and maple extract until frothy and the sugar is pretty well dissolved; should take about 3 to 4 minutes.
03. Add the coconut and pecans and stir in until evenly coated.
04. On baking sheet, form cookies with about 2 to 3 tablespoons (30 to 45 mL) of batter each, 2 inches (5 cm) apart. The mounds need to be nicely packed, not loose, so they hold together in the oven.
05. Bake for 20 to 30 minutes or until as golden as you like them, rotating pans at the midway point for even browning.
06. Allow the cookies to cool completely on the pans before attempting to lift them, or they may crumble . . . oh no! . . . and then you'd have to eat your mistake! Once completely cool, store in an airtight container for up to 3 days. Ha! Good luck with that. These babies are addictive!

macaron versus macaroon

A *macaroon* is a cookie made of egg whites, sugar and coconut. It's chewy, golden and delicious.

A *macaron* is a fussy French confection comprised of two discs of tinted and flavoured meringue with a layer of buttercream in the middle.

They are not the same thing, not by a long shot. And the names are not meant to be interchangeable. I'm not being a fusspot stickler, I'm just trying to save you from the embarrassment of being corrected by a haughty French *pâtissier* . . . in front of your date!

bonnie gordon's royal icing

MAKES ABOUT 2 CUPS (475 ML)

This is the magical stuff used to ice those super-flat and glossy cookies; it goes on liquid and dries rock-hard. My friend Bonnie Gordon runs a confectionary college and she's shared her foolproof recipe. Recipes often call for egg white powder, but I don't like that because you know it's made from factory eggs. Here we're using fresh backyard egg whites and, according to Bonnie, "When making recipes with fresh egg whites you may have to make adjustments to achieve the desired consistency; add a touch more fresh egg white if the icing is too stiff and dry, or more icing sugar if it is too soft and does not hold a peak."

If your eggs are backyard or farm fresh, there's no need to worry about consuming them raw. If you're not comfortable with that, you can use meringue powder, available in most grocery stores.

2 free-run egg whites
5 cups (1.2 L) sifted icing sugar,
    or as needed for texture
1 tsp (5 mL) fresh lemon juice

01. Ensure all utensils are clean and grease-free. Use a drop of lemon juice and a fresh tea towel to give everything a wipe.

02. Using the whisk attachment of a stand mixer or electric beaters, beat egg whites to stiff peaks.

03. Switch to the paddle attachment if using a stand mixer, and gradually add sugar until it's all incorporated. Add the lemon juice. Continue to beat on high until smooth and about the consistency of cake batter, about 5 minutes.

04. To make picture-perfect decorated cookies, use a piping bag to draw an outline around each cookie. Allow the outline to dry, then thin out the icing slightly and use it to fill in the centre of the cookie. Once the centre is completely dry, you can pipe details on top using a thicker icing.

Flood or pipe tinted royal icing onto buttery sugar cookies (page 68) for almost-too-pretty-to-eat sweet treats! These beauties were made by one of the talented bakers from the Bonnie Gordon College.

bonnie gordon's sugar cookies

MAKES ABOUT 2 DOZEN COOKIES

Bonnie's sugar cookies are so buttery-good they're almost shortbread!

2 cups (475 mL) unsalted butter, room temperature
2 cups (475 mL) sugar
1 tsp (5 mL) fine sea salt
2 tsp (10 mL) pure vanilla extract
2 free-run eggs
6 cups (1.4 L) flour
1 Tbsp (15 mL) baking powder
2 tsp (10 mL) 3.5 percent milk
1 tsp (5 mL) lemon zest (optional)

01. Preheat oven to 325F (160C) and line a baking sheet with parchment.
02. In the bowl of a stand mixer or with a wooden spoon, cream the butter, sugar, salt and vanilla until very light and fluffy. Blend in the eggs one at a time, scraping down the bowl after each addition.
03. In another bowl, blend the flour and baking powder; add to the creamed butter and egg mixture. Add the milk and blend to incorporate. Add lemon zest if desired.
04. Mix the dough until it comes together in a smooth ball. Form dough into 2 flat discs and wrap with plastic wrap; chill in the fridge for 2 hours.
05. Remove dough from fridge 30 minutes before rolling. Roll out dough onto floured surface or between two sheets of parchment paper; should be about ¼ inch (0.6 cm) thick.
06. Cut into desired shapes and transfer to baking sheet. Chill in the fridge for 15 minutes before baking; this reduces shrinkage. Re-wrap dough scraps and return to the fridge to rest and chill for 15 minutes before rolling and cutting again.
07. Bake until just set with very little colour change, about 10 to 15 minutes. Allow to cool on the baking sheet, then transfer to a cooling rack. Do not ice until completely cooled!

swiss meringue

MAKES ABOUT 4 CUPS (1 L)

• •

Like French meringues on page 71, the Swiss variety are made from just egg whites and sugar, but this time whipped in a bain-marie. This recipe is silkier, semi-cooked and used to make outstanding buttercream icing.

6 free-run egg whites
1½ cups (350 mL) sugar
1 tsp (5 mL) vanilla extract

01. In a double boiler or bain-marie (see sidebar on page 47), add egg whites and sugar to a bowl you've cleaned out with a drop of vinegar or lemon juice. The water underneath should be simmering.

02. With an electric beater, whisk on low speed until the sugar is completely dissolved and a candy thermometer reads 160F (71C); remove the bowl from heat.

03. Increase beater speed to high and continue to whip until the meringue has cooled and reached stiff-peak stage, about 5 to 7 minutes.

04. Beat in the vanilla, and if using to make Swiss meringue buttercream, use immediately while soft and silky.

italian meringue

MAKES 3 CUPS (710 ML)

• •

This is the fussiest type of meringue, edging into candy-making territory with precise temperatures required and cooked sugar syrup added to already whipped whites. Use this meringue to ice cakes, make buttercreams and top filled pies.

1 cup (250 mL) super-fine (berry) sugar
⅓ cup (80 mL) water
5 free-run egg whites, at room temperature
¼ tsp (1 mL) cream of tartar

01. In a small pot over low heat, combine sugar and water. Swirl the pot over the burner to dissolve the sugar completely. Do not stir.

Increase the heat and boil to soft-ball stage (235–240F or 113–116C), using a candy thermometer for accuracy. Wash down the inside wall of the pot with a wet pastry brush. This will help prevent sugar crystals from forming around the sides, falling in and causing a chain reaction. Prepare your meringue.

02. In the bowl of an electric mixer, whip the egg whites on low speed until foamy. Add the cream of tartar, increase the speed to medium and beat until soft peaks form.

03. With the mixer running, pour the hot sugar syrup in a thin stream over fluffed egg whites. Beat until the egg whites are stiff and glossy.

french meringue

MAKES 10–12 INDIVIDUAL MERINGUES

The simplest type of meringue, just egg whites and sugar. It ends up crunchy and crumbly, and is used most often to make dessert nests or cups for fruit and custard and such, often piped into shapes before baking. This is also the classic lemon meringue pie topping.

4 free-run egg whites
Up to 2¼ cups (530 mL) icing sugar

01. Preheat oven to 200F (95C). Line a baking sheet with parchment paper, or lightly butter and dust with cornstarch or icing sugar. I prefer the parchment method.

02. Add the egg whites to a large bowl that you've wiped clean with a drop of vinegar or lemon juice. Using an electric beater on medium speed, whip until foamy.

03. Begin adding the sugar a bit at a time and continue to beat on medium speed until stiff and glossy. I like to give it a taste because my sweet tooth isn't very strong; I don't add all the sugar but you might like things a bit sweeter.

04. Here you can go either fancy or free-form. For fancy, transfer the mixture to a large piping bag or plastic freezer bag with one bottom corner snipped off and pipe the meringue onto the prepared baking sheet in whatever shapes you desire.

05. For free-form, simply use a spoon to dollop, slightly flatten and spread piles of meringue onto the prepared baking sheet in the shapes and sizes you desire.

06. Pop the sheet in the oven and bake for about 3 hours or until the meringues lift from the sheet easily and feel completely dry and light. Some chefs suggest propping the oven door open just a smidge so it doesn't overheat; you know how precise and well-behaved your oven is, so use your own judgment.

07. Remove from oven and let cool completely before storing, or they may soften again. Store at room temperature in a covered container.

super-speedy pavlova

Top a simple French meringue with a generous dollop of Light and Fluffy Citrus Curd (page 111) and a drizzle of raspberry sauce or fresh seasonal berries. To make an easy berry sauce, just remember it's about **1 cup (250 mL) of fruit** to **3 Tbsp (45 mL) sweetener** (honey, maple syrup, sugar, icing sugar, agave) and a couple of glugs of fruit brandy, kirsch, triple sec, or other boozy component! Heat for about 5 to 10 minutes, then blend or serve as-is; do you like it rustic or refined?

tip

Snow white is pretty, but for special occasions, meringue can be tinted with food colouring.

simple savoury soufflé

SERVES 2

This is the sort of dish that can help you win friends and influence your rich uncle, and if you're the nervous type could drive you to drink. Still, it looks fancier and more difficult than it actually is. Nevertheless, I recommend practicing on your less critical friends before inviting the boss over for crab soufflé. This is the most basic soufflé recipe; once you've mastered it, try adding all sorts of deliciousness: cheese, shellfish, greens, chocolate . . .

2 Tbsp (30 mL) butter, plus more for greasing
   the dish
Bread crumbs for dusting the buttered dish
2 Tbsp (30 mL) flour
½ tsp (2.5 mL) sea salt
White pepper to taste
¾ cup (180 mL) organic 3.5 percent milk,
   cow or goat
4 free-run eggs, separated
2 free-run egg whites
¼ tsp (1 mL) cream of tartar

01. Preheat oven to 375F (190C). Liberally butter a 4-cup (1-L) round, high-sided oven-safe casserole dish or proper soufflé dish and add a good handful of bread crumbs (seasoned is nice). Rotate the crumbs around the sides, just as you would to flour a buttered cake pan. Set aside somewhere cool.

02. In a medium saucepan over low heat, melt the butter. Using a whisk, mix in the flour, salt and pepper.

03. Continue to whisk constantly and allow to cook until fully incorporated, smooth and bubbling a bit.

04. Add the milk and increase heat to medium-low. Bring to a gentle boil, whisking continuously; at this point it should be thick and smooth. Remove from heat.

05. Beat the egg yolks in a medium bowl, then add about ¼ cup (60 mL) of the warm white sauce while whisking continuously to temper the yolks. Still whisking, add another ¼ cup (60 mL) of the warm sauce, then add the rest of the sauce to the tempered yolks. At this stage, you can mix in any flavouring ingredients you like—finely minced herbs or grated Parmesan, for example. Set aside to cool down a bit.

06. In a large bowl with electric beaters or in the bowl of a stand mixer with the whisk attachment, beat the 6 egg whites and cream of tartar until stiff peaks form.

07. With a spatula, fold a big scoop of the egg whites into the white sauce, then fold in the rest of the whites. Be very gentle from this point on; until the damn thing is on the table, your only goal in life is to not collapse the egg whites! Gently and carefully pour the batter into the prepared dish.

08. Gingerly slip the soufflé into the oven. Yell at anyone who walks with more weight than a cat stalking a mouse, and bake until puffed and lightly golden—about 20 to 25 minutes. Rush to the table and serve immediately to grateful oohs and aahs.

simply sweet soufflé

It's pretty much the same as the basic savoury soufflé. Just **omit the salt and pepper** and add about ½ cup (120 mL) sugar and the **seeds of a scraped vanilla pod** to the flour and butter at the beginning. Also, when you butter the dish, use **sugar** to dust the inside of the dish.

ginger rhubarb crumble with fresh ginger fool

SERVES 8–10

When my big old ex-bat, Ginger, died, I buried her in the vegetable garden right behind a raised bed. Over her, I planted rhubarb. I decided at that moment that the next time I cooked with rhubarb there had to be ginger in the recipe. A touch macabre or sweetly sentimental? Perhaps a bit of both, but that's life, *non?*

CRUMBLE TOPPING

1 Tbsp (15 mL) softened butter for greasing
    the pan, or more if needed
1 cup (250 mL) all-purpose flour
1 cup (250 mL) packed brown sugar
½ cup (120 mL) rolled oats (not quick cooking)
1 tsp (5 mL) cinnamon
2 tsp (10 mL) ground ginger
¼ tsp (1 mL) fine sea salt
½ cup (120 mL) cold butter, cut into
    tablespoon-sized chunks

FILLING

2 free-run eggs
⅓ cup (80 mL) 35 percent cream
1 cup (250 mL) pure maple syrup
⅓ cup (80 mL) cornstarch
¼ tsp (1 mL) fine sea salt
7 cups (1.6 L) thinly sliced rhubarb,
    bitter green tops trimmed
Zest of 1 lemon

01. Preheat oven to 350F (180C). Butter an 8-inch (20-cm) square oven-safe dish and set aside. Don't fret if you don't own a baking dish this size; an inch or two bigger, round or rectangular is fine too.

02. Make the crumble topping: in a large bowl stir together the flour, brown sugar, oats, cinnamon, ginger and salt.

03. With a pastry cutter (or 2 dinner knives), cut in the butter until the mixture is blended and crumbly, and a bit sticks together when you pinch it. Set aside while you make the filling.

04. In a large bowl, whisk the eggs, cream, maple syrup, cornstarch and salt until smooth. Add the rhubarb and lemon zest and stir to combine.

05. Pour the rhubarb mixture into the buttered baking dish and sprinkle the topping over as evenly as you can. Don't worry if the dish seems too full; the crumble will sink as it cooks.

06. Pop it in the oven and bake for about 50 to 60 minutes, or until the crumbly top is golden and bubbles of pink syrup are erupting around the edges. I like to set the dish on a cookie sheet or place a sheet of aluminum foil underneath in case there's any sugary drippage.

07. Once baked, set on a rack to cool for about an hour. It needs a bit of time for the juices to thicken and the custard to set; otherwise you'll end up with something too runny, and nobody likes a soggy crumble. Serve with a dollop of my Ginger Fool (opposite).

ginger fool

MAKES ABOUT 2 CUPS (475 ML)

••

Fool is a curious name for whipped cream with fruit mixed in; it may well be frivolous, foolish even, but there's nothing silly about it—it's seriously delicious!

1 cup (250 mL) 35 percent cream
1 Tbsp (15 mL) icing sugar
1 tsp (5 mL) maple extract
2 Tbsp (30 mL) peeled and grated fresh ginger
¼ cup (60 mL) finely minced candied ginger

01. In a large bowl with electric hand beaters or in the bowl of a stand mixer with the whisk attachment, add the cream, sugar and maple extract. Beat on medium, then creep up to high until the soft-peak stage—should take about 3 minutes.

02. Add the fresh and candied ginger and give it one last whiz—just a second or two!—to incorporate.

03. Keep cold until serving.

tip

When I grate ginger, I use a rasp-style grater or Microplane. This method almost purées the ginger and makes for the most even distribution within the recipe.

SIGNE LANGFORD PHOTO

The dearly departed Ginger now nourishes the rhubarb patch.

chef christine cushing's easter tsoureki

MAKES 3 LOAVES

••

Tsoureki is a traditional Greek Easter egg-bread recipe, a gorgeous golden braided loaf with dyed-red Easter eggs baked right in. Chef Christine Cushing shares her recipe and reminiscences about a Greek childhood Easter: "My grandmother came from the beautiful island of Crete at a time when there wasn't much wealth or excess, and despite that she was so particular about everything she ate and impressed upon me at an early age how important the quality of the ingredients was. Our tradition of dyeing Easter eggs and making this fragrant, delicious Easter bread started for me when I was a teenager and Yia Yia (that's Greek for Grandma) told me about how different the eggs were in Crete. I don't think I fully appreciated that until I first went to cooking school in Paris and then on my first visit to Crete a decade ago.

"Easter isn't Easter unless I make this bread," says Chef Cushing, who was born in Greece, raised in Canada and has proudly served as the family keeper of this Easter tradition since the age of 12. "I used to camp out in sleeping bags in the living room with my cousins so we could set the timer and sleep between risings—it took me all night."

4–4½ cups (950–1060 mL) all-purpose
    flour, divided
1 tsp (5 mL) sea salt
1½ tsp (7.5 mL) ground *mahlepi* (cherry stones),
    available at specialty Greek stores
1 tsp (5 mL) ground *mastiha* (hardened resin
    of the mastic tree), also available at specialty
    Greek stores

Zest of 1 lemon
Zest of 1 orange
⅓ cup (80 mL) warm water (about 98F/37C)
¾ cup + 1 Tbsp (180 + 15 mL) sugar, divided
½ oz (14 g) active dry yeast
½ cup (120 mL) warm 3.5 percent milk
    (about 98F/37C)
4 free-run eggs, divided
⅓ cup (80 mL) melted butter
About ¼ cup (60 mL) chunky sugar
    for a final sprinkle (optional)

01. Preheat oven to 350F (180C). Line 3 baking sheets with parchment paper and set aside.
02. In the bowl of a stand mixer using the dough-hook attachment, or in a large bowl with a wooden spoon, combine 4 cups (950 mL) flour, salt, mahlepi, mastiha and the zests.
03. In a small bowl, combine warm water, 1 tablespoon (30 mL) of the sugar and yeast; stir and let stand 5 minutes or until frothy.
04. Meanwhile, in a medium bowl, whisk together warm milk, 3 of the eggs, remaining ¾ cup (180 mL) sugar and melted butter; set aside.
05. Add yeast mixture to flour mixture and blend on low speed, or stir to combine.
06. Add the egg and milk mixture to the flour and yeast and continue to mix (on low) until dough is sticky and begins to come together.
07. Turn the dough out onto a well-floured

continued on page 79

surface and knead, adding more flour as required; the dough may not require the full amount of flour. It should be smooth and elastic but slightly sticky to the touch. The process should take about 10 minutes.

08. Place in a well-buttered bowl, cover with plastic wrap or a damp tea towel and let rise in a draft-free area at room temperature for 90 minutes, or until doubled in size.

09. Punch down and transfer to floured counter. Gently pat into a rough rectangle of about 7 × 23 inches (18 × 58 cm). Cut dough lengthwise with pastry cutter or knife into 9 equal strands.

10. Working with one strand at a time, gently hold each end and tap like skipping rope on the counter until slightly and evenly stretched. Repeat with 2 other strands, then braid the 3 strands together, tucking the ends under to fasten. If desired, place red-tinted hard-boiled eggs (*kokkina avga*; see sidebar for instructions) between the strands of the braids. Transfer braid onto a baking sheet. Repeat with remaining dough to form 3 braids, each on a separate baking sheet.

11. Cover with a floured tea towel and let the braids rise in a warm place for about 50 minutes, or until the dough does not spring back when pressed with a fingertip.

12. Beat remaining egg and brush egg wash over loaves. If desired, sprinkle with sugar while egg wash is still wet; coloured sugar would be fun for the kiddos and very festive.

13. Bake loaves on middle rack of preheated oven for 35 minutes, or until golden and hollow when tapped on bottom.

making traditional greek red easter eggs

The traditional Greek way to make red Easter eggs (*kokkina avga*) is to boil them up in a whack of onion skins, so I suggest you plan on making a big pot of onion soup or caramelized onions, which are fine for freezing, canning or eating on just about anything! Or—and don't tell Yia Yia—do what I do, and use beet juice or red wine.

SHE'S A REAL MOTHER HEN

summer

THE SUMMER CHICKEN AND GARDEN

THE EGG: SUMMER RECIPES

the summer chicken and garden

All chickens are descended from a wild Asian jungle fowl, so hot and humid is where they come from, but our chickens today are wildly different from their ancestors and, just like us, get a little wilted when it's killer hot outside.

Still, they like a little sunshine, just like you and me; and the first time you come out into the yard to find one of your hens collapsed, wings drooping, legs splayed, feathers all standing up on end, head back and eyes glazed, don't panic.

Karen Bertelsen, the blogger behind *The Art of Doing Stuff*, with Walnut, her Rhode Island Red and Ameraucana cross, inside the fabulous coop she built with her bare hands. Or maybe they were gloved. Still, impressive!

PHOTO COURTESY KAREN BERTELSEN

Sure, she might look like roadkill, but she's just sunbathing. You will quickly get used to the sight of it—this is what chicken bliss looks like.

THE ART OF KEEPING COOL

Steeltown, The Hammer, Hamilton . . . call it what you will, this blue-collar Ontario town is enjoying a bit of a makeover, courtesy of artists and hipsters driven out of Toronto by untenable housing costs. It's a city with more going on than meets the eye, from a burgeoning farm-to-table foodie scene to urban backyard hen-keeping.

The gal of all trades behind *The Art of Doing Stuff* blog, and a hen-keeper since 2011, Karen Bertelsen shares her backyard in Hamilton with four lovely ladies and their stunning, sleekly urbane black and white coop (see page 164)—built by Karen herself, natch!

Hamilton is in Zone 6, which is chilly—not Alaska chilly, but chilly enough—so Karen's readers are often curious about how her hens weather the cold. "What people don't realize is that the cold isn't going to kill the chickens, but the *heat* will. So even though I put a tiny ceramic wall heater in their coop two winters ago, it wasn't to keep them alive, it was merely to keep their combs and waddles from freezing. In the summer, on the other hand, I'm often out there at two o'clock in the morning checking the temperature of the coop and plugging a fan in to make sure they don't get overheated. When your chickens are panting, it isn't a good sign and they really can just drop dead from heat."

Chickenade for Hot Chicks

Ever feel like you're just going to keel over unless you get an ice-cold sports drink down your gullet ASAP? I do after several hours of garden work; sometimes it's the only thing that will restore the body's balance after a ton of sweating. Well, even though they don't sweat—they really are such ladies!—hens also benefit from an electrolyte drink when it's blisteringly hot out or when recovering from a scare, illness or injury. In fact, hen-keeper Lisa Steele advises, "Replacing the electrolytes lost during times of oppressive heat could mean the difference between life and death to your chickens." Here's her recipe for a homemade electrolyte supplement.

> 1 cup (250 mL) water
> 2 tsp (10 mL) sugar
> ⅛ tsp (0.6 mL) fine sea salt
> ⅛ tsp (0.6 mL) baking soda
>
> Mix all ingredients together and give full-strength to severely ailing chickens. For healthy birds, add to their drinking water as needed: 1 cup (250 mL) of concentrate per 1 gallon (3.8 L) of water.

GROW UP!

A hen will eat what she can reach. And if something looks particularly yummy, she'll jump to NBA-calibre heights. If I forget and leave the garden gate open, my tomatoes end up with beak-shaped puncture wounds. So, if building fences

dairy and the ladies

Some say yea, some say nay, I say every now and then is okay. I'd even recommend a wee dish of probiotic plain yogurt for basic upkeep of healthy digestive tract flora and fauna. In the summer when it's hot outside, I'll add a handful of frozen blueberries for a cooling, nutritious treat.

like ice cream for chickens

Just like everyone, chickens enjoy a cool treat in summer. Lots of hen-keepers make special foods for their ladies at different times of year. I make hen-porridge in the winter and in summertime freeze berries, herbs, peas, corn kernels and edible flowers in ice as a fantastic way to keep the girls cool and entertained. If you use a Bundt pan you can then hang the frozen ring, even more fun for them. You can also use ice cubes to add to a bowl of drinking water.

I also hang whole heads of lettuce in summer and cabbage in winter. Drive a hole through the middle and string it up!

is not an option for you, vertical, hanging and raised gardens are all good ways to maximize growing space and protect edibles.

climbing beans: When choosing bean varieties to plant, pick pole rather than bush varieties.

cucumbers: These vigorous growers do well in pots and climb like mad over arches and up trellises or strings. My girls have shown no interest in them; squirrels, on the other hand, beat me to half my crop!

endless summer

I look at some folks and can't help but think, "Man, they've got it all figured out!" Like Jenny Carcia and her Pet Chicken Ranch. Jenny lives in Petaluma in Sonoma County on California's northern coast; that's a toasty Zone 9 for those of you keeping track. She keeps a small flock—Buff Orpingtons, Barred Rocks and Easter Eggers—that get to free-range in comfort 12 months a year. Still, there are seasonal challenges, and when the weather turns scorching, Jenny takes extra measures to keep her ladies from overheating.

"In very hot weather—anything above 85F (29C)—I add ice to my hens' water around midday, and may even put out an extra watering station. We have the coop under a large pine tree, excellent protection from the summer heat. Our first year keeping hens, the coop was in the sun and quite miserable in the summer."

She also keeps a close eye on her ladies: "If any of the hens look heat-stressed, I bring them in the house so they can cool down as quickly as possible. Cool water, good airflow and lots of shade are important in hot weather. We put ice packs in the nest boxes on hot days. I will even hold a hen in my lap along with an ice pack right up against her to cool her down. They are spoiled hens living in an environment that isn't too extreme—we are all very lucky."

Spoiled indeed! I thought my hens were spoiled, but now that I've met Jenny and her flock of prima donnas I'm feeling a little like Mommie Dearest!

But why shouldn't she spoil them? Jenny is an artist, and her hens her muses. Using textiles, wire, stuffing and fluff, she magically captures the nuances of character of her subjects in the gorgeous fabric-art chickens she creates.

In a warm climate, hygiene takes on an extra degree of importance, simply because there is no downtime or off-season. Pests grow and multiply year-round. "The floor is covered with large wood shavings and cleaned lightly every single day and completely renewed with wood shavings every two to four weeks."

On the plus side, the California heat also means she and her ladies enjoy an extended garden season. "Over the years we have grown many different things for the hens, but have finally landed on sunflowers. We grow as many as possible in the summer, and then feed the dried seeds to the girls throughout fall and winter."

Jenny Carcia, the artist behind the Etsy store "Pet Chicken Ranch," in her California studio with a few of her fabric flock (top). One of Jenny Carcia's adorable bespoke hens. Jenny works from photos to create each hen in fabric, wire and florist tape (bottom).

hanging strawberry planters: So pretty and practical, although the sweet red berries may—oh, who am I trying to kid—*will* still fall prey to squirrels, raccoons and birds.

melons and zucchini: Smaller varieties can be trained up well-secured trellises; the melons will need a little extra support as they grow.

peas: Another tasty climber to consider; so far, my backyard peas have not tempted the ladies in the least.

upside-down tomatoes: In hanging planters (or buckets), tomatoes will look novel, and based on how well they grow, don't seem to mind this turnabout one bit.

Beautiful Nugget. She was a proud, bossy little gold Sebright—a true bantam breed—no bigger than a pigeon, with the silliest song and biggest personality.

pots or plots, plant lots

I plant mega amounts of marigolds for their stinky pest-repellent properties and because the ladies love to eat the leaves. And I always plant lots and lots of nasturtiums: I love the variety of flower colours, the look of the leaves—solid or variegated—and how they act as aphid magnets. I call the ones I plant around my vegetables "sacrificial nasturtiums," as they draw sap-sucking baddies away from veggies (and roses). The ladies love nasturtiums too. So I plant climbing and trailing: some for me, some for them. The unopened flower buds can be brined into "capers," the leaves and flowers are tasty and beautiful added to salads, and the seeds are very easy to collect and dry for next season's crop. And when the ladies chow down on the bug-infested leaves they get a sweet protein blast from the aphids! Plus these plants are herbal helpers; see The Ultimate Hen Herb Garden (page 14).

ITTY-BITTY BREEDS FOR MICRO-PLOTS

Don't let a postage stamp–sized plot stop you from gardening with hens. Just as there are ways to work around size limitations in gardening, there are ways around the space issue with keeping hens. Coops can be very small indeed, as long as your ladies have an attached run or will have plenty of opportunity to free-range. And there are itty-bitty breeds—bantams—just perfect for a tiny urban lot. Their peewee-sized eggs are adorable, and just as delicious as the larger types.

GIRLS' SPA DAY

What gal doesn't enjoy a little primping and pampering? I give my ladies a couple of spa days a year. This is your chance to get a good look at all

ANGRY AS A WET HEN

the bits that can cause trouble—feet, vent, skin, crop, tummy—and give everything a really good cleaning while taking care of any doctoring. But, unless you are set up to let the hen dry off inside your house, don't do this in winter; I don't advise sending a wet chicken out into the cold.

Look for a plastic-coated dishwashing apron to help keep you dry, and before you start, be sure to set yourself up with everything you need before you've got a water-logged hen on your hands . . . literally!

Here are some other tips learned the hard (and sometimes wet) way:

- Place a rubber dishwashing mat on the bottom of the sink. It gives your possibly very cranky hen something to grip onto. If her feet are sliding around a slippery sink, she'll feel more vulnerable and be more likely to flap, splash and try to escape—and you will get soaked!

- Fill up the kitchen sink with very warm water; remember that a bird's body temperature is higher than ours (about 103F or 39.5C), so the water should be a tad warmer than we might like for ourselves. A drop of natural shampoo or dish soap, a heaping handful of sea salt and a splash of apple-cider vinegar make the water extra-cleansing for hardened-on poop, dirt, cuts and scrapes.

- Before you start, set a couple of layers of old towels out for your wet hen to stand on and one for wrapping around her after the bath. Once she's all bundled up—she'll look like a chicken burrito!—you can turn her over and take a look at the soles of her feet. This is where you might find the beginnings of bumblefoot (page 136). Do her nails need trimming or is she keeping them short with all her scratching in the yard? What about the scales of her legs and feet—are they raised, lifting off and showing signs of mites (page 139)?

- If you've noticed a poop buildup on your hen's fluffy butt feathers, it's really important to soak the stuff until it's soft enough to remove without hurting her or pulling out too many feathers in the process. Not only is a poo-y butt ugly, it attracts flies, and that can lead to a horrible situation called flystrike (see page 137 for the gruesome details).

- Check around the vent for feather shafts coated with nits or lice eggs. Cut or pluck out affected feathers and burn them (but not near the coop or run!) or flush them down the drain. Die, nits, die!

- My ladies fuss a bit in the water but do they ever settle down when I set them on a towel for the foot scrub. It must feel just as good to them as it does to us. I use a wet toothbrush with a bit of soap to get in there and scrub hard, especially if they've got some raised scales from mite activity. Don't be alarmed if a few scales come away; that's good. Rinse the soapy water off, towel dry, then slather on petroleum jelly. If there are mites feasting on your ladies' gams, this will suffocate these bloodsuckers. Reapply once or twice a week—sometimes indefinitely; these little buggers can keep coming back!—to make sure

chicken craters

Dust bathing is the chicken equivalent of dry shampooing. The dry dirt fluffed down between feathers exfoliates, scratches the heck out of mites and absorbs oils and other accumulated gunk from feathers and skin. Your hens' desire to dust bathe will—note, I did not say *may*, I said *will*—turn parts of your garden into a barren, cratered moonscape. Forewarned is forearmed.

I've noticed my girls tend to favour spots with loose dry soil or sand. On a scorcher of a day, they'll look for a dust bath in the shade—the cool earth must feel lovely—and on cooler days, a combo sun-and-dust bath is hen heaven!

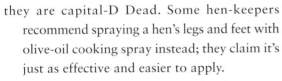

Think of dust bathing as a dry shampoo. It's necessary and they really seem to love it. It even has a unifying effect. Hens who normally torment each other are perfectly happy to loll about in the dirt right up against each other without squabbling!

SIGNE LANGFORD PHOTO

they are capital-D Dead. Some hen-keepers recommend spraying a hen's legs and feet with olive-oil cooking spray instead; they claim it's just as effective and easier to apply.

- For a final touch, a little vegetable oil or petroleum jelly on the comb and wattles makes them lovely, red and moist-looking—and I've yet to meet a gal who doesn't covet dewy skin!

PEST CONTROL IN THE GARDEN AND COOP

Chickens will consume as many bugs as they can get their beaks on: slugs, grubs, ant eggs, things that fly. And there is nothing funnier than watching a hen chase a moth, running and hopping in a frantic zigzag.

Hens can help eliminate the need for chemical pest control. When you are turning the soil, the

All I have to do is touch a shovel or pitchfork and the ladies know what's about to go down. Worms, grubs, centipedes, potato bugs, ant eggs—down the hatch!

SIGNE LANGFORD PHOTO

ladies will be right there at your feet, waiting to pounce on anything that turns up, from creepy crawlers to germinating weed seeds. A mature standard-sized hen will even hunt mice, and while I've seen the odd hen give half-hearted chase to a feed-thieving sparrow, they've not yet caught one, thank goodness!

Coop Critter Control

Sometimes, though, while hens are helping to combat garden pests, their coop can attract unwelcome guests. Mice and rats can become a problem—cozy straw and yummy feed are like an engraved invitation—especially in colder months. I believe the furry critters are just par for the course, but it's vital to control their numbers. You have a few options to keep rodents in check, some requiring extreme caution.

get a cat: Kitties and chickens can and do live well together without incident. However, I wouldn't put an aggressive feral cat in a barn, coop or run with small hens such as bantams. But a well-socialized neutered cat should do well with standard-sized hens. Best results are had when a cat is introduced to the flock as a harmless and impressionable kitten.

glue traps: A crime against all that's good and decent in this world, glue traps are indiscriminate, catching harmless garter snakes, helpful spiders, even little birdies, and cause a long, terrifying and painful death for the mice or rats they are intended for. Please don't use these. Not anywhere. Not ever.

live traps: As long as you check them every day, this is the most humane way to go, although not the most effective. Mice and rats will run right back home unless you drop them off miles away.

poison: The hardware store shelf is full of poisoned pellets, blocks, powders, pastes and grains; some work, some don't and some work too well. Rats and mice can develop resistance to certain toxins, rendering some baits no more deadly than a bad meal. Others are so powerful they leave the dead rodent as poisonous as the bait, and therefore pose a danger to other animals that may consume the corpse—including your ladies and other pets. If you do use poison, it's a challenge to find spots to place it where your ladies—or other non-target critters—won't be able to get at it. If using anticoagulants, such as warfarin, it's a good idea to check with your vet about emergency doses of vitamin K, the treatment for warfarin poisoning.

snap traps: They're basic, simple, inexpensive, reusable and do the trick quickly and, I hope, painlessly. The trouble is a curious hen could lose her beak, foot or worse. When I use snap traps, I set them only in areas the hens can't access; at night I place them in the run, when the girls are safely tucked into their coop. Just make sure to remove any un-snapped traps in the morning, before first light. I slept in one morning—and by slept in, I mean the sun beat me to it—and when I came down to disarm the traps my worst nightmare was before me: a sparrow, dead, its neck broken in one of them. I felt sick. It will be a long while before I let myself off the hook for that cock-up.

SUCCULENT WEEDS TO FEED YOUR HENS

Hens love dandelions, and just about any tender shoot, and that means weeds don't stand a chance; what they don't eat, the hens scratch up. Some hen-keepers place moveable, wire-mesh

OPPOSITE, CLOCKWISE FROM TOP LEFT: Cindy Loo in summer (SL); the Peeper contemplating the stairs (SL); a gravestone for a mated pair of budgies (SL); forget-me-nots (DG); digging is a favourite pastime (DG).

This ingenious system of wire hoop tunnels allows hens to feast on pests and fertilize while not allowing them access to the veggies. Some set-ups have one end open to the coop or run, and some have wire doors at either end to let the ladies in and out.

tunnels between rows of vegetables and let the ladies in. They'll spend some time in the row, then the gardener will move the tunnel and hens to the next area that needs weeding, de-bugging and fertilizing. Plans for these hen tunnels can be found on the internet, and are pretty simple.

EVERYONE LOVES A CHICKEN DINNER: PREDATOR PRECAUTIONS

Introducing chickens into your garden is like laying out the welcome mat for all the potential predators in your area. It's just a fact of hen-keeping. But there are ways to deal with the various critters who'd *love* to come over for chicken.

In Southern Ontario it's primarily raccoons and hawks that ruffle my feathers, and occasionally the ladies'. I'm right in the city, so foxes, coyotes and possums aren't too much of an issue, thank goodness.

So how do you predator-proof your girls? You can't, not 100 percent, but you can keep them pretty safe and make it more work than it's worth for the hunters.

raccoons: Bold, clever, determined and good climbers, and how about those agile little hands? I've seen too many first-time hen-keepers who've set up a rickety retro-fitted rabbit hutch or some other flimsy coop, only to lose their girls to a middle-of-the-night raccoon attack. When I first got my girls, I came outside one night to find six *(six!)* raccoons crawling all over their little coop. I

was freaked out. I can't imagine how terrified the girls were, with just a bit of wire between them and certain and gory death. Since then, my girls have been living in Fort Knox. Doors are latched tight. I've hung bells on the door to the run and

chickweed for chicks

The state of Alaska is massive and enjoys a variety of climates. Fairbanks, where Mara Bacsujlaky keeps her flock of chickens, is in the Alaskan interior. "We have hot summers, and our growing period is from late May to mid to late September, and because we get 20 hours of sun a day, things grow like crazy!" Mara says, "Gardens are very popular here. We grow almost everything, though tomatoes, cukes, basil and peppers do better inside greenhouses. Outside, potatoes, broccoli, greens, lettuce, beans, zucchini, peas, cabbage and Brussels sprouts all do extremely well."

Mara doesn't grow anything just for her birds; she doesn't need to, with plenty of volunteers. "We have an abundance of chickweed, lamb's quarters, fireweed and bluebells, which I pick for my hens since they are not free-range."

I'd like to mention that while Mara's hens aren't free-range, they do enjoy a large coop and run that is very open to the outdoors. But in her part of Alaska, predation is a really big issue. A big, scary, furry issue!

the coop; if a raccoon climbs on either, it jingles and The Dude—my fearless chihuahua—goes wild at the back door. Wire skirts are bolted to the ground against diggers, and a roof keeps the climbers out. So far, so good.

birds of prey: The more common hawks in my area—Cooper's and red-tailed—are big enough to kill or at least seriously injure a hen. Thankfully, these impressive raptors are fairly easy to foil. A hunting hawk needs a clear and straight path to dive down, hit its target and then get airborne again as quickly as possible. Use your love of gardening to protect your flock. Plant as many trees as your garden will support, dotted here and there throughout the yard; don't just stick to the edges. Also, use garden arches and other decorative elements—umbrellas, tables, chaises, bird baths—as obstacles to a clear flight path. And, of course, provide plenty of places for the girls to take cover.

Mara's North Country Anti-Predation Tips

In Alaska, where Mara Bacsujlaky keeps her flock, predators are a tad more formidable. She deals with foxes, weasels, bears—grizzly and black—ravens, owls, hawks, even loose dogs. "It is absolutely necessary to have a very sturdy fence around the coop and have it netted." Though, she says, "Many people do free-range their chickens and are willing to lose some to predators. There have been hen-keepers who have had their hen-house completely destroyed by bears."

Also, she advises:

- Don't leave chicken feed outside where bears can smell it; it's catnip to them!
- Get dogs—big ones!—that will bark, warn and even defend the coop.
- It's common for foxes and weasels to dig under fencing and into coops, killing an entire flock in one night. Roaming dogs will do this too. Some folks dig a trench around the perimeter

there's one in every flock: the henny penny

The Henny Penny. The one hen that sounds the alarm call at the slightest provocation, setting all the rest off in an ever-more-shrill spiral of panicked squawking—often for absolutely no good reason at all. And, no, a squirrel is not a good enough reason to send me running out into the yard barefoot in winter!

It's important to develop mother's ears for your hens' calls. Because you too will be compelled to bolt from whatever it is you're doing and run like mad to see what the matter is. It might be a cat, a raccoon or a stranger. Or it might be nothing at all. But you just don't want to take the chance.

As soon as I get outside, I scan the garden and watch my hens' eyes to try to figure out what

they might be looking at. Like I said, it's usually nothing, but once they've started setting each other off it can be quite challenging to shut them up. Food is really the surest and fastest way to end the cacophony. But not just any food. Once the ladies are officially in a tizzy, a handful of scratch won't bring them down. No, it's going to take the big guns: lettuce, cheese, peanuts, grapes. And if your ladies are anything like mine, they'll shut up just long enough to eat the treats and let you get back to whatever it was you were doing, only to start right back up again. Once a flock is on edge, it tends to stay that way for a while—threat or no threat.

of the run and coop to sink hardware cloth to a good depth, then pack it down with heavy rocks and soil.

- Death from above comes in the form of ravens, big owls, hawks and eagles—that's why covering or netting the top of the run is vital.

DO YOU SPEAK CHICKENESE?

Well, I'm better at understanding it than speaking it. A huge part of the joy I receive from keeping a flock of hens is the time I spend among them, simply being with them, observing and interacting. It's in the observing that you'll learn the most. And if you're quiet and just watch and listen, you'll soon realize they have a complex and fascinating language. And while chickens speak chicken and sparrows speak sparrow, they understand each other.

I've observed as a sparrow lets out a cry that I believe translates to "OMG! A hawk! *Everybody quiet! Hide!*" And with that call, but for the rustle of leaves and feathers, the world falls silent as every bird within a three-garden radius takes cover—including my hens. They dart under whatever is nearest as fast as their drumsticks can carry them. They'll huddle together, stock-still, heads cocked to the side, one beady eye on the sky. If you listen closely now, you'll hear a low sound coming from one, a few or all of the hens. It's somewhere between a growl, a purr and a deep trill and it means: "Shhh . . . don't move . . . don't make a sound . . . death from above." They'll continue to make that sound as long as they can see the hawk and will stay still and silent until the bird is long gone. If you keep listening,

you'll hear that the world remains hushed until every living thing feels safe again; then the garden erupts with chatter and calls of "all clear!" . . . especially from the blue jays. Oh, and they'll yak and yak about what just went down, but not the ladies. They just go back to pecking and scratching.

The more time you spend watching and listening, the more Chickenese you'll learn, from the sound they make that means "This is delish!" to "Will ya get a load of this bug I got!" Sometimes a top girl will say, "Come on over here and share this extra-tasty tidbit!" and other times a proud lady will shout, "Look at me! I just laid the most spectacular egg in all the world!" The squawk-fest that signals a nest-box war can be mistaken for a danger call and is just about the most annoying thing they get up to. Seriously, seven nest boxes should be enough for a flock of four or five, right? Wrong.

The sound of a true attack by a ground predator is unmistakeable and gets you on a primal level. I've heard that sound on a couple of occasions and simply can't recall how I went from my desk on the second floor to the backyard. One instant I was at my desk, typing, and then as if by magic I was in the garden and there was no time, space or experience in between. I can't prove it—there's no video evidence—but I think I can fly. And that's when you will find a menacing cat or raccoon and you may have to leap into Mama Hen mode.

I *do not* recommend it, but I have engaged in hand-to-paw combat with a hungry raccoon. I didn't think, I just did. Stupid, I know, but instinct is strong when you care for something as much as I care for my ladies.

Two juicy, hard-to-come-by water buffalo burgers were on the grill. I popped inside to grab

OPPOSITE, CLOCKWISE FROM TOP LEFT: Big Mamma and the Peeper (SL); nasturtium in bloom (SL); angry bird? (SL); a snuggle with Nelly (DG).

there's one in every flock: the mean girl

Living with hens can take you back. Back to the bad old days of high school. It doesn't require too many hours of observing your ladies to see the striking resemblances between a flock of hens and a gang of teenage girls, complete with all the politics and intrigue of a particularly eventful day in Grade Nine. There's all the usual squabbles over primo real estate or nibbles; there's bullying, pushing and shoving, even petty theft. And there's The Mean Girl. The Betty Rizzo, the Amber Von Tussle . . . she rules the roost, pecks the most heads and basically turns on the other hens at the drop of a . . . feather. But remove her, and The Mean Girl in Training will just move on up the ranks; so you've just got to step back and let Mean Girls be mean.

the rest of my dinner. The plan was water buffalo, salad and wine under the umbrella. I was in the kitchen for but a moment when I heard it: the alarm call. No Henny-Penny-make-a-fuss-for-nothing this time; no, this was for realz, yo.

Helen, my blind Leghorn, sat squashed flat to the ground, the full weight of an adolescent raccoon on her back. His arms and legs were wrapped around her, his teeth gnawing away on her comb. I guess if you plan to eat a chicken from head to tail, it's a logical place to start, but not on my watch and not my lovely Helen!

It was a hot day and I was in flip-flops and a sundress, not dressed for mortal combat. I'd had the mister spraying, so the ground was slick. I ran, hit the mud and landed hard on my side; now both Helen and I were bleeding. The Dude ran ahead and was barking and nipping at the raccoon, but the hungry fellow wasn't letting go of my (apparently) delicious Leghorn.

There I was—muddy, bloody, stinging from gravel burns—and I did the craziest thing *ever*. Without one single solitary thought, I grabbed the thing by the scruff of its neck. It didn't let go; it held hard, its teeth still sunk into poor old Helen's comb, which appeared to be a tad rubbery as appetizers go. I shook the raccoon, doing my best impression of Granny dislodging Tweety Bird from Sylvester's gob: "Drop it! Drop it! Drop it!" And it did. It dropped Helen, who plopped to the ground, oblivious, blood staining her pretty white feathers.

If it's fair to ascribe human-like expressions to a raccoon's face, I'd say this one looked surprised by the crazy lady and this terrible case of chicken interruptus.

But now I was standing there, my right arm fully extended, a stunned raccoon dangling from my hand. For one brief delicious moment of payback I considered bashing its brains out on the fence. But I haven't got it in me. So I pulled back, like a pitcher on the mound or discus thrower, and flung it with everything I had. Over the fence and past the neighbour's picture window it sailed.

I took a breath, but poor Helen! And my burgers!

Helen was easily mended: wash, disinfect, snuggle. The burgers were not so lucky. The glorious rare patties were now carbonized hockey pucks of broken dreams . . . but I still had the wine, and Helen. The ladies had the burgers.

the egg: summer recipes

If spring feels like waking up after a long slumber, then summer is that languid time spent with the ladies soaking up every moment of sun and bliss on a Sunday morning when you've got all the time in the world, nowhere you have to be and nothing more pressing than to gather the day's rich summer eggs and select the perfect vine-ripened tomato for lunch.

It's cucumbers plucked prickly from the vine, sliced, drizzled with cider vinegar and sprinkled with sea salt, the way Father dished them up. It's warm cherry tomatoes that burst candy-sweet in my mouth, my treat for dutifully pinching off the suckers every morning despite the leaves kicking up a stink in protest. And it's that first cup of tea early in the morning, when the city is still quiet, my girls at my feet or perched on the arm of my chair, pecking and preening. All this as I ponder delicious ways to keep the ladies—and myself—cool through another afternoon of back-yard abundance.

MATTHEW COOMBES PHOTO

Baby Marlowe somewhat reluctantly sharing her watermelon with Helen, a blind rescued Leghorn.

ted reader's mucked UP eggs

SERVES 2

Ted Reader is a man of extremes. An extreme cook—the man can plank anything. An extreme collector—at last count, he had somewhere in the neighbourhood of 50 grills, barbecues and smokers in his backyard. An extreme author—now at 21 books on the art of the grill. *And* an extremely nice guy. So nice, in fact, he's shared his dad's special egg recipe with all of us! Now, Ted's recipe calls for duck eggs, but chicken eggs are just fine.

He writes: "My dad was a good cook. He didn't cook a ton but when he did it sure was delicious. There were a few recipes of his that I loved: His holiday turkey dinner (it was the best), his live-fire grilled steaks (that's what got me hooked on grilling) and this breakfast dish called Mucked UP Eggs! My dad made this recipe for me on special-occasion weekends when I was younger but as I grew older he also made them for me when I woke up a little hungover! A mucked-up egg is two soft-boiled eggs spooned over diced buttered toast and then mucked up with a spoon. This is my updated version of this classic family recipe."

I dare say this is Ted's *extreme* version of a classic family recipe.

3 Tbsp (45 mL) butter, plus extra for toast
1 small sweet onion, finely chopped
2 cups (475 mL) sliced white or brown mushrooms
2 tsp (10 mL) finely chopped fresh flat-leaf parsley
1 scallion, finely chopped
8 slices smoked bacon, coarsely chopped
Sea salt, freshly ground pepper and cayenne
    pepper to taste

4–6 slices bread, toasted: white, brown, rye,
    challah or any kind you want
4 free-run eggs
Dash hot sauce, your favourite brand

01. Melt the butter in a skillet over medium heat. Sauté the onion and mushrooms for 10 to 12 minutes, or until golden brown, stirring occasionally. Remove from heat and add to a large bowl.

02. Add the parsley and scallion to the bowl and toss with the cooked mushroom mixture.

03. Return the skillet to medium heat and fry the bacon until crisp. Add the bacon to the bowl and stir. Taste and season with salt, pepper and cayenne pepper. Set aside to keep warm.

04. Toast the bread until golden brown, butter and dice into ½-inch (1.25-cm) cubes; add to the bowl and toss with all the other ingredients. Return to a warm spot while you boil the eggs.

05. Soft-boil the eggs in enough water to cover. See Hard-Boiling: My Way (page 26) for how to make a perfect soft-boiled egg.

06. Spoon equal amounts of the bacon and mushroom mixture into 2 wide-mouthed beer glasses or mason jars.

07. Carefully remove the egg from its shell and spoon over the bacon and mushroom mixture. Add hot sauce to taste, serve immediately and let the eater do the mucking up! Suggested beverage: an icy cold brew or spicy Caesar.

tip

For the jarred roasted peppers, I like
Chef Christine Cushing's Fired Up brand;
it's sweet and spicy and smooth as silk.

spicy egg puff squares with mascarpone and nduja

MAKES 4 SERVINGS AS AN APPETIZER OR 2 AS A MAIN

These are so easy and elegant—an assembly job really—and they're creamy and spicy and totally impressive-looking on the plate with a side of simple greens for brunch or lunch.

½ cup (120 mL) mascarpone, at room temperature

¼ cup (60 mL) nduja, at room temperature, casing removed

5 free-run eggs, divided

1 sheet all-butter puff pastry, thawed according to package directions

4 tsp (20 mL) roasted red peppers in olive oil, mild or spicy

Finely chopped fresh basil, chives or flat-leaf parsley for garnishing (optional)

01. Preheat oven to 400F (205C).

02. In a medium bowl, add the mascarpone and nduja and blend well. Set aside.

03. With a fork, beat 1 egg in a small bowl.

04. Place a length of parchment paper onto the counter, and very lightly flour the paper. Unfurl the pastry out onto the floured paper and, with a floured rolling pin, roll the dough out just a tiny bit to stretch it another 1 to 2 inches (2.5 to 5 cm) in length. Lift the paper with dough onto a baking sheet.

05. With the tip of a sharp paring knife, cut the sheet of pastry into 4 squares. Turn up the edges of each pastry square to form a lip and pinch at the corners to keep in place. Brush the edges of the pastry squares with the egg wash and prick the bottom of the squares all over with a fork.

06. Divide the mascarpone mixture between the 4 squares. Spread out a dollop of cheese in each square, and make a depression in the centre to cradle the egg.

07. Crack an egg into each depression and sprinkle about 1 tsp (5 mL) of the roasted peppers on top of each egg. If you have any runaway whites, just lift up the pastry edge and make that wall higher!

08. Bake for 10 to 12 minutes, or until edges are puffed and golden and the yolk is starting to set. Sprinkle with chopped herbs if you choose, though it's pretty flavourful as is.

---

puff inspiration: Well, sort of a variation, but really more of a tip and a license to thrill. Once you have mastered thawing and baking puff pastry from a box, you can pretty much top it with anything—sweet or savoury—and come off looking like a freakin' genius! Try this: unfurl the puff, place it on a parchment-lined sheet, cake pan or roasting pan. Spread with a nice layer of Crème Anglaise (page 51), stopping 2 inches (5 cm) in from the edges. Now here's where you can do whatever makes you happy: top with thinly sliced fruit; sprinkle with berries, grapes, raisins; dollop with jam; or simply dust with cinnamon or shaved chocolate. Now into the oven to bake.

hangry eggs

SERVES 1 HANGRY PERSON

The weirdest things stay with me.

Exhibit A: that scene in *Shirley Valentine* when she serves her unappreciative "Where's me steak?" hubby a plate of chip 'n' egg.

Two things: dear lord, there's not a scrap of green anywhere in sight. Not a lettuce leaf, not a sprig of parsley. And that struck me as rather an unfortunate meal. I may well have asked poor downtrodden Shirley where my steak was too!

Fast forward 20 years or so. I now understand the delight of crispy, salty fried potato with runny-yolk fried eggs. This is my go-to hangry (so-hungry-I'm-angry) meal, especially when I've been working non-stop in the garden, too in love with the springtime sun and smell of warm earth to come in and eat when I should. No, I work and work and work until I'm beyond hungry: dizzy, frantic and *hangry*.

I don't make chips—I rarely break out the deep fat—but I do love rösti. When the potatoes are from my own patch, all the better, but either way this is super-fast, simplicity itself, delicious and so pretty. This is a meal for one because any bigger and the potato takes too long to cook to qualify as a hangry meal. If you want to make it for two or more, you will either need more time or individual cast iron skillets—which, by the way, are all the rage these days, brought right to the table for eating out of.

1 large potato, red skin or Yukon Gold, scrubbed and eyes removed
4 tsp (20 mL) olive oil, divided
2 tsp (10 mL) butter
1 or 2 free-run eggs
Sea salt and black pepper to taste, divided

01. Grate the potato with the large-holed side of a box grater; set aside.

02. Set a 6- to 8-inch (15- to 20-cm) cast iron skillet over medium heat. Add butter and 2 teaspoons (10 mL) oil to the skillet, melt and tip around the pan.

03. Add the grated potato to the hot oiled pan and press it down evenly and all the way out to the edges of the pan. Sprinkle with salt and pepper.

04. Fry for about 5 minutes or until it's becoming crispy and golden; take a peek under an edge every now and then to make sure the potatoes aren't getting too dark.

05. When the first side is a lovely golden brown, drizzle the uncooked side with the remaining oil and flip the potatoes. Crack an egg or two on top—depending on how hangry you are—and season with more salt and pepper.

continued on page 102

SIGNE LANGFORD PHOTO

06. Cook the eggs as you like; I like runny yolks. Pop a lid on—or use my bottom-of-the-hot-kettle trick (page 30)—to make sure the egg is ready at the same time as the second side of the potato. Should take about 7 to 10 minutes on medium heat.

07. Set the pan on a wooden board and serve with a non-synthetic tea towel around the handle, a loud warning about how hot the pan is, and feel free to bring the bottle of HP to the table. Oh, and Shirley gave his steak to the dog.

cheesy hangry eggs: Grate some of your favourite cheese and top the cooked potato and egg with it. Pop it under the broiler until the cheese is all bubbly good, though the yolks will now be hard-cooked.

oniony hangry eggs: Grate an onion along with the potato, mix it up and complete the recipe as usual.

crispy bacon hangry eggs: Chop and fry a couple of strips of bacon or slices of ham in the potato pan until just softened. Add the potatoes and complete the recipe as usual.

corny hangry eggs: If you have some cold, firm polenta kicking about, switch it up with the potatoes. Just cut the polenta into sticks and fry as you would the potato rösti. Complete the recipe as usual. Polenta goes seriously crunchy and it's super-delicious with the eggs.

An onion in full bloom!

salade niçoise with an ontario twist

SERVES 2

Composed salads sound fancy, but they're really just ingredients arranged on a plate, either per person or on a family-style platter. This classic from Nice, in southern France, is wonderfully malleable and can be given all kinds of twists by changing up an element or two. But whatever you add, take away or tweak, it makes for light and easy summertime eating and entertaining. Hard-boiled eggs are traditional, but when a yolk is as spectacular as your own backyard yolks, *mollet* or semi-soft is my preferred way to show them off.

VINAIGRETTE

1 small shallot, finely minced

¼ cup (60 mL) cold-pressed hemp oil
(or substitute extra-virgin olive oil)

2 tsp (10 mL) apple-cider vinegar

1 tsp (5 mL) maple mustard (or substitute
Dijon mustard)

1 Tbsp (15 mL) maple syrup

Freshly ground black pepper and coarse sea
salt or fleur de sel, to taste

SALAD

20 skinny wax or green beans, or a mix
of both, stem-ends trimmed

8 new potatoes, scrubbed

2 free-run eggs

10 assorted heirloom cherry or teardrop
tomatoes, halved

6 oz (170 g) smoked Ontario trout, broken
into a few large pieces

½ cup (120 mL) mixed olives in oil
(be sure to include some Niçoise)

6 fine-quality Spanish anchovies in olive oil
(optional)

01. To make the vinaigrette, add the shallot, oil, vinegar, mustard, syrup, pepper and salt to a bowl and whisk, or add into a lidded jar and shake to emulsify. Set aside.

02. To blanch the beans, bring a shallow pot of salted water to a boil, drop beans in and cook for exactly 1 minute. Lift out and transfer to a bowl of icy water to chill and shock in the vibrant colour. Once completely cool, set aside in a colander to drain.

03. Bring a pot of salted water to a boil, tumble in the scrubbed potatoes, reduce heat and boil gently until just fork-tender—about 10 to 12 minutes depending on the size of the potatoes. Drain and set aside to cool and dry. Once cool enough to handle, cut in half.

04. You can boil the eggs in the same water as the potatoes; just put them in the simmering water for 6 minutes, then transfer to a bowl of ice-cold water. When that cold water turns warm from the heat of the eggs, refresh with more cold water until the eggs are chilled right down. Peeling is a delicate operation, best done under a gentle drizzle of cold running water.

05. Now simply arrange all the ingredients on a platter or divide between 2 plates. Drizzle with dressing and serve with a crunchy-crusted locally baked loaf made from Ontario grain and a lovely bottle of something pink, cold and bubbly . . . preferably from Ontario.

tips for preparing raw fish

If you're not familiar with preparing raw fish, here are a few things you'll want to know:

- Make this recipe in a non-reactive bowl, such as glass, Pyrex, glazed earthenware or plastic.
- Keep the fish cool up to the last minute.
- When purchasing the fish, ask your fishmonger for sushi-quality or sushi-grade wild or organic farmed fish. Tell them it's for eating raw, so it must be super fresh.
- Ask them to let you give it a sniff before they wrap it up. You shouldn't smell anything— not fish, nothing but the ocean blue! And don't be afraid to reject a piece of fish you wouldn't feel completely happy eating raw.
- Ask them to skin it for you or do it yourself with a very sharp boning knife.
- Ask if they have already removed the pin bones. Still, when you get home, run your hand over the piece of fish, feeling for pin bones; there may be a stray or two. Use tweezers or needle-nose pliers to pull them out.

sushi-style fish tartare with brûléed yolk

SERVES 2

This dish was hugely popular wherever I cooked. Magically, it's light and rich at the same time, and the bright flavours of toasted sesame, soy and pickled ginger are super-refreshing with the ice-cold fish. In my restaurant, we kept salad plates in the fridge; if you've never tried this at home, do. There's really something special about enjoying crisp greens or, in this case, raw fish from an icy surface, and that doesn't have to be a plate. I've served food on cold blocks of Himalayan pink salt, terra cotta tile, glass and slate. Offer some wasabi paste on the side if you like a blast of head-clearing heat!

A note about the fish: choosing a sustainable, ethical fish is getting harder and harder. For this recipe, stick with something fairly safe and uncomplicated, such as wild-caught Arctic char or Canadian-farmed trout. Salmon trout has a rich, fatty flesh, very close to its namesake.

8 oz (225 g) sushi-quality pink cold-water fatty fish, skinned and chopped into ½-inch (1.25-cm) dice (should be about 1 cup/250 mL)

3 scallions, finely chopped

½ cup (120 mL) finely diced English cucumber

4 tsp (20 mL) finely chopped pickled ginger (preferably without artificial sweeteners)

1 tsp (5 mL) soy sauce

1 tsp (5 mL) mirin

¼ tsp (1 mL) toasted sesame oil

1 tsp (5 mL) seasoned rice vinegar

½ tsp (2.5 mL) black sesame seeds

1 free-run egg yolk

½ tsp (2.5 mL) vanilla sugar

Pinch wasabi powder

01. Into a non-reactive bowl, add the fish, scallions, cucumber, ginger, soy sauce, mirin, sesame oil, vinegar and sesame seeds. Stir together to blend, then cover and pop back into the fridge to chill before serving.

02. While the tartare is chilling, mix together the vanilla sugar and wasabi powder in a small dish; set aside.

03. When it's time to serve, place the tartare on a chilled platter and make a depression in the centre to cradle the yolk. Slip the yolk into the depression, top the yolk with the sugar-wasabi mixture and brûlée with a kitchen torch.

04. Serve immediately with something crisp—Japanese rice crackers, toasted baguette or deep-fried wonton wrappers. This dish is made even more special when served with a little chilled sake or Japanese plum wine on ice.

decadent orange cream

SERVES 2

Virgin or boozalicious, either way I think you'll love this frothy summer drink. To me, it tastes somewhere between a Creamsicle and an Orange Julep.

There was an Orange Julep stand at the Fairview mall when I was growing up, and since the mall was a good 30-minute drive from home, it was a real treat when Father would buy me one. I loved the frothiness of it—didn't everyone? It was a mystery then; I now know the secret is egg whites. This recipe takes me back, but now I'm old enough to add a healthy splash of vanilla vodka to it . . . no trip to the mall required!

Now, I'm going to be a stickler about this one; if you don't have eggs fresh from a backyard lady and you don't have freshly squeezed orange juice, DON'T bother! You will not love it! Seriously.

2 free-run eggs
2 cups (475 mL) cold freshly squeezed orange juice
2 Tbsp (30 mL) runny honey
2 oz (60 mL) chilled vanilla vodka (optional)

01. Put all ingredients into a blender and blend until foamy. Garnish with a little slice of orange and serve immediately.

RULE THE ROOST

rich and dark eggy almond iced dream

MAKES ABOUT 3 CUPS (710 ML)

• •

I adore ice cream but live a life of ice cream depriva-tion. I have to, because if I didn't, I'd happily eat the stuff morning, noon and night, seven days a week. I know this because this is what happens when a tub enters the house. And that is why I simply can't have the stuff around, and why I own an ice cream maker instead. You heard me. One of my favourite kitchen toys is my Donvier Ice Cream Maker by Cuisipro—in hot pink, no less! It's a simple hand-cranked gadget that actually works. I plop some organic Greek yogurt and maple syrup into it whenever I feel a craving coming on and it does the trick. I even use it to make the real thing too, once in a blue moon.

I make this brilliant recipe with chocolate almond "milk"—that stuff is loaded with calcium!—good dark cocoa and my ladies' eggs to make it super-rich and velvety. I prefer Almond Breeze Chocolate Almond Milk; it works well, doesn't separate and has a nice amount of chocolatey flavour to start with.

As a bonus, this stuff is versatile. When first made and still warm, it makes an amazing hot fudge sauce, and poured into little cups and chilled, it's the richest chocolate pudding ever.

3 free-run egg yolks

1 free-run egg

2½ cups (600 mL) chocolate almond milk

2 Tbsp (30 mL) butter or coconut butter

½ cup (120 mL) maple syrup

¼ tsp (1 mL) fine sea salt

½ cup (120 mL) dark cocoa powder
(I like fair trade cocoa)

01. In a large bowl, whisk the egg yolks and egg until well beaten; set aside.

02. In a medium saucepan over medium-low heat, add the almond milk, butter, maple syrup, salt, and sift in the cocoa powder (to eliminate any lumps). Bring to a gentle simmer, stirring often to prevent sticking and burning. Simmer for about 5 minutes, stirring often, then remove from heat.

03. Temper the eggs: add a tiny bit of the hot almond milk to the beaten eggs a few drops at a time, while whisking like mad. If you add the hot almond milk too fast or don't whisk fast enough, you'll end up with sweet scram-bled eggs. Keep at this until you've added about half of the hot almond milk mixture to the eggs.

continued on page 110

If you don't have an ice cream maker, this recipe can be poured into little cups and chilled to make a rich chocolate pudding.

04. Pour the tempered eggs back into the saucepan with the rest of the almond milk mixture while whisking. Return to low heat and simmer for 5 minutes, stirring constantly, until the custard has thickened a fair bit. Remove from heat. It may seem too liquid, but it will thicken further as it cools.

05. If you want to be sure to remove any small pieces of cooked egg, set a fine sieve over a bowl and pour in the custard. Personally, I never bother (I like to live on the edge!), but some folks—far fancier than I—would insist! Put the lovely, satiny custard into the fridge to chill for at least 3 hours or up to 24 hours. This is important; you need to start with ice-cold ingredients or your home ice-cream maker might not be able to cope and you'll have runny ice cream.

06. When custard is cold, add to your machine and follow the manufacturer's directions. The one I have just takes a few minutes of elbow grease and some patience—no need to scream—for ice cream!

black cherry chocolate iced dream: For a black cherry variation, stir in **1 cup (250 mL) frozen coarsely chopped black cherries** to the mixture before chilling.

dark chocolate espresso iced dream: For a mocha variation, add **2 tablespoons (30 mL) instant espresso powder** along with the almond milk.

greek yogurt iced dream: To go probiotic, simply whisk in **¼ cup (60 mL) plain probiotic Greek yogurt** to the chilled custard before adding it all to the ice-cream machine.

light and fluffy citrus curd

MAKES 1½–2 CUPS (350–475 ML)

The only lemon curd I tasted growing up came out of a jar. The grocery store kind was, and often still is, starchy, dull and overly sweet. When I made my first batch of homemade, it was mind-blowingly rich, tart and just so much better than anything out of a jar—even a jar all the way from England.

It's one of those things that can be used in a number of ways: in a trifle, in tarts or tartelettes, between layers of cake, as a dessert topping, and on and on. It's also a great gift, packed into pretty little jars.

On super-hot days I'll put some curd in a bowl, tumble in some frozen blueberries and gently stir them in. After about 5 minutes in the fridge, the blueberries have softened just enough and it's all wonderfully refreshing.

I call my version "lighter" because I use whole eggs, while most recipes call for just the yolks; I find the whites give a lighter, fluffier, prettier, pale yellow curd.

Go ahead and use any combination of citrus juice you like: lemon and lime, orange, blood orange and lemon . . . I also call for vanilla sugar, which isn't the norm but I love that combination of lemon and vanilla. Feel free to use regular sugar if you prefer.

½ cup (120 mL) vanilla sugar

½ cup (120 mL) freshly squeezed citrus juice

Zest of 1 lemon or other citrus fruit

4 free-run eggs

6 Tbsp (90 mL) butter, at room temperature, cut into chunks

01. Into the top part of a double boiler or bain-marie (see page 47 for instructions), whisk together the sugar and juice. The water should be simmering, not boiling. And be sure to use a whisk, to whip air into the curd.

02. It's important to keep a close watch on the heat; the temperature of the sugar and lemon should never be too hot, just warm. Carefully feel the sides of the bowl or double boiler—if it's too hot, you will end up with a batch of sweet, lemony scrambled eggs.

03. If you want to be on the safe side, keep another pot or bowl to the side of the stove, full of ice water. If your mixture gets too warm, just rest the bottom into the ice water and whisk like mad. That will bring down the temperature in a hurry.

04. Now add the eggs and get ready to stand there and whisk vigorously for the next 20 minutes or so. Keep whisking and scrape down the sides with a rubber spatula so you don't end up with a lot of overcooked curd clinging to the bowl or pot.

05. Once the mixture is starting to resemble curd—about the thickness of yogurt—whisk in the butter, one chunk at a time.

06. Once all the butter has been added and the curd is lovely and smooth and thick, set it aside to cool uncovered and at room temperature. Once it's fully cooled, you can cover and store in the refrigerator.

teeny tiny lemon meringues en coquille d'oeuf

MAKES ABOUT 15 MERINGUES

This dessert is about as sweet and adorable as a fluffy baby chick, and absolutely perfect for brunch. Once you decide you're going to make this, you'll need to start being very mindful about how you crack open the eggs you cook with; you'll need to save up as many perfect shells as you wish to serve, with just the right opening near the top. If patience is not one of your virtues, go ahead and boil up as many as you need and make some egg salad!

Serve the filled shells in egg cups with wee spoons—avoid silver—and a few simple all-butter, not-too-sweet shortbread cookies. This recipe is also a perfect excuse to buy one of those nifty kitchen torches; you'll need one to brûlée the meringue. If you're not into the eggshell thing, any tiny vessel will do—espresso cup, liqueur glass, shot glass, sake cup, you get the idea—but the size will change and so will your amounts.

1½ cups (350 mL) Light and Fluffy Citrus Curd, chilled (recipe on page 111)
1½ cups (350 mL) French Meringue, recipe on page 71
⅓ cup (80 mL) vanilla super-fine or regular sugar

01. Prepare 2 dozen eggshells to be used as serving cups (see sidebar for instructions). Place in serving cups and set aside.
02. Fill the prepared shells with chilled lemon curd; set aside.
03. Top each filled shell with a nice tall dollop of meringue, or get all fancy and pipe it on. Sprinkle each with a wee bit of the sugar and brûlée with a kitchen torch. You can also try it under the broiler, but it can be tricky and tippy and I don't recommend it.

how to prepare eggshells for use as serving vessels

Invest in an egg topper or another sharp eggshell-cutting tool specifically designed to cleanly slice the tops off boiled eggs. I have one from Swissmar that does the job. It works well with boiled eggs, either soft or hard, but with raw eggs, it tends to shatter the shell. Once you've got nice empty shells, rinse them out with *cold* water. If you use hot, you'll cook any remaining egg right onto the shell. Once it feels completely clean inside, and you've pulled out any bits of membrane, turn the shells upside down to drip dry.

froufrou chocolate chiffon cake

SERVES 8 TO 10

Mother had her specialities: a menu of a handful of sweets and savouries she'd only do for company. She made a *baba au rhum* that took a full day of drenching in rum so it soaked it all up. She'd make it when her friends Max and Nancy were over for dinner— he swooned over the booziness of it and Mother swooned over Max's attention and compliments. I watched all of this with fascination, especially the final few splashes of warm rum she'd pour over the cake while she was getting dressed for the party. Standing at the dark-brown stove in pantyhose with a few curlers still bobbling on her head, she'd dip her measuring cup into the pot of rum and melted apricot jam and pour it over the sponge-like baba that seemed to have an endless capacity for more rum. This throat-burning, yeasty, not-nearly-sweet-enough cake was a cruel trick to play on a kid.

But *this* cake—her magnificent pale chocolate chiffon cake slathered in deep drifts of soft-beige whipped cream—met all of my expectations and more. Most astonishing was the depth of whipped cream, and the way she filled the centre cavity, top to bottom, with even more whipped cream—I'd never seen such decadence, such abandon, such a girly, froufrou confection. I've made it more summery, with a healthy slathering of raspberry whipped cream, a smear of extra jam and a nice pile of fresh berries.

RASPBERRY WHIPPED CREAM

3 cups (710 mL) 35 percent cream
2 Tbsp (30 mL) super-fine (berry) sugar
⅔ cup (160 mL) homemade raspberry jam
  (or excellent-quality store-bought),
  plus extra for garnishing

2 tsp (10 mL) pure vanilla extract
Pinch fine sea salt
½ cup (120 mL) fresh raspberries, for garnishing

CAKE

½ cup (120 mL) loosely packed pure cocoa (I like
  fair trade)
½ cup (120 mL) boiling water
½ cup (120 mL) neutral vegetable oil
½ cup (120 mL) buttermilk
2 tsp (10 mL) pure vanilla extract
6 egg yolks, at room temperature
1¾ cups (415 mL) sifted cake flour
2 tsp (10 mL) baking powder
1 tsp (5 mL) fine sea salt
1¼ cups (300 mL) packed brown sugar
7 egg whites, at room temperature
½ tsp (2.5 mL) cream of tartar
½ cup (120 mL) sugar

01. Preheat oven to 325F (160C) and adjust the oven rack to the bottom third of the oven.

02. Add all of the raspberry whipped cream ingredients to the bowl of a stand mixer with the whisk attachment and start beating on low, gradually increasing the speed to medium-high. Whip until soft peaks form. Cover and set aside in the fridge until ready to ice the cake.

03. In a small bowl, whisk the cocoa powder with the boiling water until perfectly smooth. Add the oil, buttermilk and vanilla to the cocoa

continued on page 116

liquid and whisk to combine. Whisk in the egg yolks.

04. Into a large mixing bowl, sift the flour, baking powder and salt. Add the brown sugar and stir, crushing any lumps. Add the chocolate liquid mixture to the flour mixture and stir just to combine. Do not over-work or the batter will be tough.

05. Wipe out a large bowl or the bowl of a stand mixer with a drop of lemon juice or vinegar. Using the whisk attachment, beat the egg whites on medium speed until frothy. Add the cream of tartar to the egg whites, increase the speed to medium-high and continue to whisk until soft-peak stage. Reduce speed to medium and gradually add the sugar, then increase speed back up to high to firm, glossy peaks.

06. Add about a third of the whipped egg whites to the chocolate batter and gently fold to incorporate. Add the remaining egg whites and very gently fold in to evenly incorporate.

07. Pour the batter into an ungreased angel food cake pan and bake in the lower third of the oven for about 55 minutes. The cake should bounce back when touched and a skewer inserted near the centre should come out clean.

08. Transfer baked cake to a cooling rack to cool completely before removing from pan. When cool, run a knife around the edges, then invert directly onto serving plate; you don't want to handle it too much.

09. Now, some folks like to slice this tall cake

into layers and spread the whipped cream between all the layers, but I leave it whole and fill the centre hole with cream. First drop the raspberry whipped cream into the middle, one spoonful at a time. Then use a spatula to spread the rest of the cold whipped cream all over the top and sides.

10. Use the back of a spoon to spread a little more raspberry jam over the top of the cake, then pile up with fresh berries. Serve immediately or pop into the fridge to set; the whipped cream will soon slide and fall at room temperature.

îles flottantes

Food writer, television host, cookbook author and francophile Laura Calder may have cracked the code to a happy life, having spent much of it between her current home of Toronto, her "spiritual home" of France and her childhood home of New Brunswick. I couldn't think of a better person to turn to for a classic French egg dish. And, I might add, she tells a heck of a story too.

"It's easy to become jaded when it comes to classic dishes. I was, until I went to France and ate my way through the classic French repertoire. Time and time again, I found myself tasting something I assumed would be boring, only to feel like I was tasting food for the first time in my life. I couldn't believe all the marvellous dishes I'd been missing out on my whole life!

"So it was, too, with îles flottantes. I was in my twenties in Normandy, I remember, visiting one of the beaches. It was a steel-grey wind-swept day, the kind of weather that creates just the right mood for melancholic thoughts about the war and the stupidity of all that loss. There was a little restaurant somewhere down near the water, sort of a shack-like affair, and I went in for a bit of lunch to cheer myself up. I don't remember my first course and I'm equally blank about the main. All I know is that I ordered floating islands for dessert. I never order dessert, so who knows why I did that day, but it turned out to be one of the most shockingly good things I think I've ever eaten.

"Never underestimate the dreaminess of a thick, silky and very cold custard made with a vanilla bean, for one thing. Now, imagine a lake of that topped with swan-white marshmallowy clouds of delicately poached meringue and ornate golden shards of caramel that shatter at the touch of your spoon. It was an indulgence. And, let me tell you, when you sit eating something that heavenly in a place on earth that has been the site of such hell, you really want to savour every mouthful with slow respect. You almost want to stand up and salute the dish, in fact, to salute all classics, because such are dishes definitely worth fighting to preserve."

Laura's recipe is based on Linda Dannenberg's from *Paris Bistro Cooking*, and she calls for a final topping of caramel, but since I'm a raving nationalist and proud Canadian, I'm going to finish this dish with a sweet drizzle of pure perfection: Canadian maple syrup!

6 cups (1.4 L) 3.5 percent organic milk, divided

1 vanilla bean, split lengthwise and scraped

5 free-run eggs, separated

6 Tbsp (90 mL) sugar

Pinch fine sea salt

¼ cup (60 mL) super-fine vanilla sugar

⅓ cup (80 mL) maple syrup

¼ cup (60 mL) dark spiced rum

continued on page 119

Light-as-air soft meringues poaching in vanilla-infused milk. Only do a couple at a time; they can be tricky to flip!

01. For the custard, put 2 cups (475 mL) of the milk in a medium saucepan over medium heat. Add the scraped vanilla seeds to the milk, then drop the bean into the pot. Bring to a simmer, then remove from heat, cover and leave to infuse 10 minutes.

02. In a medium bowl, whisk the yolks with the sugar.

03. Stirring quickly, add a spoon or two of the hot milk to the yolks to temper. Still stirring, add another couple of spoonfuls, then add it all into the saucepan with the milk. Pull out the vanilla bean and set aside for the poaching step.

04. Return the milk and yolk mixture to medium heat and simmer, stirring with a wooden spoon, until it thickens enough to coat the back of a spoon. Do not allow to boil or the custard will curdle. Cool completely, cover and chill. You can make the custard the day before if you wish.

05. For the meringues, bring the remaining 4 cups (950 mL) of milk to a simmer in a large deep skillet along with the reserved vanilla bean.

06. With hand beaters or a stand mixer using the whisk attachment, whisk the whites and salt to stiff peaks. Add in the vanilla sugar and keep beating until glossy, firm peaks form.

07. Working in batches to avoid overcrowding the milk, use a large spoon to scoop out a total of 8 meringues and lower them into the simmering milk. Poach for 1½ minutes on one side, then flip and poach for a further 2 minutes. Remove with a slotted spoon to a clean, lint-free dishcloth to cool.

08. In a small saucepan, bring maple syrup and rum to an exuberant simmer. Simmer for about 10 minutes; it will thicken as it cools.

09. To assemble the dessert, pour some custard into a shallow serving dish. Arrange the meringues on top and drizzle with maple syrup mixture.

autumn

THE AUTUMN CHICKEN AND GARDEN

THE EGG: AUTUMN RECIPES

the autumn chicken and garden

For gardeners and hen-keepers, autumn is bitter-sweet. In the vegetable patch, you're still bringing in the late ripeners, and in the flower beds the fall bloomers are giving the bees one last chance to feast before the first killing frost. For hens, it's a time of kicking around in newly fallen leaves and helping themselves to anything left behind in the garden. Once I've taken everything I want to take from the fenced-in parts, I open the gates and let the ladies in. Like a gang of rock fans, they rush for festival seating!

Fall is a subtly pretty time in the garden, with warm orange tones, fiery reds, and greens fading to yellows and browns. The air and light feel different, with a certain sweetness on the breeze and golden glow in the sunshine. The sunchokes have reached their peak—some have made it to 15 feet—and still bear bright yellow flowers, grabbing as much last-minute sun as they can to plump up the delicious tubers waiting below. Almost frantic, bumblebees go from one bloom to the next, then on to the masses of purple asters and goldenrod.

In the kitchen, thoughts and cravings turn to steamy pots of soup, preserving and aromas of baking. Outside, it's time to get the garden, coop and run ready for winter.

TIDY UP AND TUCK IN

The shift to the chilly seasons in most parts of North America used to be fairly predictable—steady cold with a good snow cover in some places—but not anymore. Climate change is causing extreme fluctuations, surprising weather events and wild storms. In winter the best thing for the garden is consistent cold with a lovely insulating blanket of snow. A heat wave in March, while momentarily pleasant, wreaks havoc with buds. And wind plus cold without snow cover equals dehydration (freezer burn) and dieback.

The best we can do for our garden is to wrap our beloved evergreens, Japanese maples, roses, shrubs—especially fruit-bearing—with burlap. Mounding them up at the base with soil and applying a deep layer of mulch or straw (not hay) is also helpful. And don't forget a few super-soaks to the roots before it starts to freeze at night.

SO MUCH MULCH

Some mulch—that coloured chunky stuff sold in bags at landscaping shops—is just so ugly and I don't think it does a lot of good. I've seen weeds germinating between those golf ball–sized orange lumps and that big stuff would be next to useless

Lizzy Borden was one of two gorgeous redheads; Ginger was the other. Both were rescued egg-factory hens, both had horrible starts in life, both narrowly escaped a terrible death and both went on to live and lay for another five years.

in a chicken garden, offering little in the way of protection to garden beds. They would enjoy kicking it around though!

But I understand the value of proper mulch—water retention, weed suppression, nutrient delivery—and use it around plantings. But what do I use? Well, I've got an endless supply of poop-enriched bedding from the coop to spread around liberally! The only drawback is the odd bit of grain that remains in the straw to sprout; but then again, as soon as it germinates, it's gobbled up to be processed into compost via my hens! Here are some further mulch possibilities:

coffee grounds and loose tea leaves: Save them yourself and perhaps talk to your local coffee shop about collecting more for you. The ladies may ingest a tiny bit, but not enough to harm them.

newspapers: I love using newspaper (printed with vegetable ink, of course!). I like to put it through a shredder and then either place it in the coop and nest boxes—to be composted at a later date—or add it to the compost directly.

nut shells and other stuff: And there are more and more commercial by-products coming from all over the world, all the time. Some are ways to turn waste into revenue and others clever ways to deal with invasive species; the Australian paperbark tea tree or melaleuca (*Melaleuca quinquenervia*), for example, is spreading through Florida at an alarming rate, so the Florida forestry folks have teamed up with private enterprise to turn the stuff into mulch. Bottom line, do your research to ensure you are making an eco-sane choice.

pine needles, leaves and grass clippings: It just kills me to see bags of garden "waste" by the side of the road! I know the city is going to do something useful with it, but I'd as soon put a bag full of organic matter at the curb as I would a bag of gold! I will keep my biomass for myself, if you don't mind. And you should too! Use this material as mulch or, even better, toss it into the compost. Just remember what each material brings to the party—brown or green, acid or alkaline—and keep it in balance.

I started some radish sprouts in eggshells; when the sprouts were big enough to make a nice snack, I just gave the whole lot to the girls. They ate the sprouts and the shells.

sawdust and woodchips: Pine smells lovely, and as it breaks down it adds organic matter, nutrients, beneficial lignins and tannins, and increases water-holding capacity to the soil. However, only go with sawdust if you are 100 percent sure it's from wood that is not chemically treated.

EGGSHELLS *ARE* ALL THEY'RE CRACKED UP TO BE

I know I don't need to tell gardeners to save and compost eggshells. But there are a few more ways to get the most from these beautifully formed calcium bombs:

a slug's worst nightmare: Blend shells into a coarser powder with lots of sharp, jagged bits and sprinkle around the garden against slugs and other of their creepy ilk. Death by a thousand cuts. Die, slug, die!

back from whence it came: I like to roast up a batch of shells until they're brown and brittle. I pop them into the blender and pulse them into a crumbly powder to add back to the girls' feed or sprinkle on top of their treats, such as watermelon. If a hen is calcium deficient, she'll pull it from her bones and muscles to make eggs, leading to weakness, bone breaks and egg binding. I roast the shells because of the concern that feeding hens eggs and eggshells will cause them to become egg eaters. I'm not convinced, but I still do this just in case; it's easy and takes no time. And yes, I still do toss the ladies a whole fresh egg every now and then, and not one of my girls has yet to let her appetite for eggs lead her to a life of crime.

biodegradable seed pots: Start seeds in eggshells. If you're a big eater of soft-boiled eggs, you'll accumulate the right kind of shells fast. If not, you'll have to perfect your egg-cracking technique to take off only a small portion of the pointy end when you add them to recipes. And you'll need to save or ask friends for egg cartons.

Set the empty shells into a carton, fill each with potting soil and seed. The shells won't leak water, so they're safe for your windowsill. When it's time to transplant into the ground, there's no need to remove the shell; just give it a squeeze or tap on the bottom to fracture it a bit. The roots will do the rest and the little plant has a ready source of minerals and calcium.

eat 'em: Seriously, don't we all hate crunching down on a stray bit of shell in our scrambled eggs? And here I am suggesting you eat shells on purpose. But as a powder, shells are easy to sneak into meals. Wash shells well, roast, then powder in a blender or spice grinder. Add to smoothies, hot oatmeal, even pancakes! It's good for you and your dog, cat or pet bird, too. But, and I can't stress this enough, do *not* use factory eggs for this, and roast long enough to kill bacteria: 30 minutes at 350F (180C) will do it.

eco-cleaner: Ground-up eggshells are abrasive and can be used to scrub pots and pans. Make sure the shells are powdered finely and it shouldn't be an issue for the plumbing.

eco-facial: We already know eggshells are abrasive when ground up or powdered. Finely powdered washed shells can work like the most expensive skin scrub and won't poison the lakes and oceans with toxic microscopic plastics. Buzz in the blender, then take the shells to the next level of powder with a mortar and pestle. Mix the shell powder with a bit of coconut butter, olive oil, dairy (yogurt, kefir) or honey; scrub and rinse to face the world all dewy!

get crafty: Kids and adults can have some fun playing and getting creative with eggshells. I've seen beautiful jewellery made with dyed eggshell and, of course, what kiddie hasn't decorated eggs? Filled with beeswax and a little wick, they make cute candles, and washed and dried they make stylish minimalist houses for air plants.

Wouldn't these be lovely on an Easter brunch table? And when the wax is gone, compost the shell.

get dishy: Give eggshells a second life in the kitchen; clean them inside and out, and use as chocolate moulds or cute serving dishes for a rich, delicate bite of savoury custard or sweet mousse (see Teeny Tiny Lemon Meringues en Coquille d'Oeuf, page 112). For this, you'll want to invest in a little kitchen gadget called an egg "topper" or "cracker"; there are also egg-topping scissors, but they don't work nearly as well. The topper cuts the top off smoothly and evenly.

in coffee: Folks are very, *very* serious about making coffee nowadays. The pour-over method is king! But, when I was growing up, most moms and dads used a percolator. My mother always put an eggshell in the percolator, which sat on the stove, heaving, sighing and bubbling away, cooking up what I can only imagine was a rather bitter brew. With all its sighing and moaning, Mother called it "the sexy coffee pot"—that was self-explanatory, but why did she put the eggshell in? Seems it's founded in good science; eggshells are alkaline and coffee is acidic. The shells help reduce some of the bitter acidity when brewing with this old method.

plant with tomatoes: Blossom-end rot in tomatoes is caused by calcium deficiency. Simply add some eggshell powder to the bottom of your freshly dug hole when planting tomato plants or, better still, start tomato seeds in eggshells!

THE CUTEST WALKING GARBURATORS EVER

Hens are walking garburators that produce both food and fertilizer. Give them kitchen scraps and let them visit the compost pile; they'll aerate, eat bugs and leave their own nitrogen-rich calling card behind. Add used straw bedding to the compost and garden beds. Raked up from the coop and run, it's full of poop, feathers and often diatomaceous earth—a slug's worst nightmare! In fact, chickens are so effective when it comes to composting that the wee village of Pincé, France, without a budget for a municipal composting program, instead supplies each household with two hens a-laying. Kitchen waste goes in, eggs and fertilizer come out. How civilized!

SOIL MANAGEMENT HEN-STYLE

Hens spend most of the day pecking, scratching, eating and pooping. In other words, aerating, practicing pest control and fertilizing the soil.

straw versus hay: what's the difference?

Straw stalks are hollow (you know, like a drinking *straw*?), so they trap air, making them a superior insulator. The trouble is, those hollow straws also make excellent hidey holes for mites and other creepy crawlers. In the compost or spread on the garden, straw is fine, as it tends to not have any seeds (grains) left.

Hay, on the other hand, is greener, full of seeds and, since the stalks aren't hollow, not as good for winter bedding . . . but, then again, pests don't hide in it as easily. It's a tough choice! My ladies love a fresh bale of whatever I give them, and if there are grains to glean they're over the moon! In winter I favour straw for warmth. I've heard some chicken experts say a big N–O to hay since it is so green and moist and therefore prone to moulds. One more thing: be mindful of where you purchase your bedding. In the fall when your local hardware, grocery or garden shops display straw or hay for Halloween décor, many of these bales will have been treated with a nasty fire-retardant chemical . . . so ask.

This is just hens being hens. You can put them to work as the happiest garden helpers you'll ever have. When I have to spread fresh soil onto my beds, I simply leave piles dotted around and let the ladies go to work; they'll break the mounds down, spread it and pick it clean of insects and weeds. I do a final raking to smooth it out. Um . . . they'll "help" with that too, by redistributing what you've just raked into place, so best to do this once the girls are in the run. No matter how many times I tell them they've helped enough, they insist on doing more.

Ashes to Ashes

I have a small barbecue-cum-firepit that I use to burn up scraps of wood and twigs. The ash is good for both hen and plant health. I sprinkle the cold ash on my garden beds, confident that the ladies will find it and pick at it or roll around in it. If you have an indoor fireplace, that ash is good too, as long as you're not burning those weird faux woods or chimney-cleaning chemical logs. Pure natural charcoal is a detoxifier and filter. But:

- Never burn chemically treated wood.
- Never burn anything near the coop or run.
- Never sprinkle ash in the coop or run; one warm ember and it's game over!
- Never sprinkle even slightly warm ash anywhere; it can blow around, find a bit of dry straw, and tragedy!

THE SCOOP ON POOP

Hen poop is nitrogen-rich and, when fresh, too hot for tender seedlings. Compost it with leaf litter or other brown material—straw, kitchen scraps, a little newspaper, the contents of your office shredder—or make manure tea (see Hen Poop Tea, page 127). As a hen-keeper, it's important to become a poop connoisseur. Hen droppings can tell us so much about the health of our ladies; the colour and texture can indicate health—good or otherwise—and their droppings may reveal the presence of blood or worm eggs or segments. The internet is a rich source of scatological information and images of the good, the bad and the ugly.

tip

Don't want to brew poo for your houseplants? I bring in one perfectly formed green hen dropping from the coop to add to each of my houseplants—just pop the poop in the pot!

Hen Poop Tea

Gag, I know, it sounds disgusting, but your plants think tea brewed from hen poop is as yummy as a G&T.

Using a ratio of one part poop to four parts water, let the brew sit in the sun—cooler weather slows down the process but still works—and give it a stir every now and then. By the next day or so, you'll have a nourishing plant tea. You can make more concentrated tea by steeping it for longer—up to two weeks—and diluting it before applying.

OMG, what is that disgusting poop?

There's chicken poop and then there's chicken poop from hell. Okay, maybe not hell exactly, but close enough: from the ceca (I think that's Latin for Satan's latrine) or cecal pouches. The ceca play a role in the absorption of nutrients from more difficult to digest materials, recycling nitrogen from urates and basically fermenting the food. When the ceca expel their own special brand of waste it is enough to make you question your affection for chickens. And, for some mind-boggling reason, this is the poop you always track into the house, which means you have to . . . well . . . burn the place down. Thank goodness each hen only produces a couple of stinkers a day, and if you watch where you walk, they are easily identifiable because they look evil. Rule number one of cookbook writing is *never include pictures of poop*, so you won't find a photo of one here. Google "cecal chicken poop" and don't say I didn't warn you.

After a year or so of adding goodies to the top, I opened up the little sliding door at the bottom of my composter and out poured the loveliest, blackest soil ever—my thrill-level was so high, I realized I was a biomass junkie.

SIGNE LANGFORD PHOTO

carbon to nitrogen ratio

Every gardener knows a thriving garden is the result of a brilliant balancing act. This balance is super-important in the composter too. When composting hen poop, try for a 20:1 ratio of carbon to nitrogen. Hen poop is nitrogen heavy, as are tea bags, coffee grounds, lawn clippings, weeds and food scraps. Carbon sources include dry leaves, used henhouse bedding, paper printed with eco-friendly inks and chemical-free waste from the woodworking shop.

A BIOMASS CONFESSION

My name is Signe and I am a biomass addict . . .

I hate the idea of anything that can be transformed into soil leaving my tiny bit of land. I have two large compost piles and the only precious stuff that still leaves my house does so via the plumbing and city green-bin program. Until recently, newspaper was dropped at the curb for recycling, but since I purchased a second-hand shredder, it now gets composted along with the straw and hay after spending some time keeping the gals comfy-cozy in the coop.

PLANT A CROP OF GREEN MANURE

Some cover crops are planted to fix nitrogen in the soil, and some have beefy taproots that can help bust up hard-packed and clay soils. When the green tops are tilled or dug back into the soil in the early spring, other nutrients and mass are added too. Save some greens for your ladies!

alfalfa: A nitrogen fixer and large biomass producer that breaks up compacted layers, limits erosion and improves soil permeability.

buckwheat: Good at pulling phosphorus from the soil and a great weed suppressant or "smother crop," as well as a pollen source that attracts honeybees and other beneficial insects.

cowpea, clover, vetch, lupine, fenugreek and other legumes: These cover crop superstars add enough nitrogen to the soil to feed whatever you plant in that spot the next season. They also encourage soil biodiversity and attract many beneficial insects. I sow my raised vegetable beds with clover in late fall, then close the gate and don't let the ladies back in until the big spring cleanup.

mustard, daikon, radish and other brassicas: Their strong taproots can help bust up heavy, compacted or clay soils. At the other end of the spectrum to legumes, brassicas are nitrogen scavengers, which is great if your garden beds are rich in hot manure. If you've got hens, you've likely got a surplus of hot manure. Bonus: most hens love brassicas.

sorghum and sudangrass: Outcompete weeds for sun and water, encourage beneficial nematodes and create a good amount of biomass.

S.O.S. (SAVE OUR SEEDS)

Fall is the time to collect all seeds for sowing next spring or for trading with fellow gardeners—and it's good to get this done before the rough weather starts. Wait for a few sunny days in a row and then collect only fully ripe dry seeds. Just remember, moisture is your enemy when it comes to seed storability. Don't put lids on anything until you're 100 percent sure the seeds are completely dry. Save those silica gel packets that come in boxes of new shoes and in food and vitamin packages to slurp up any stray moisture inside your jars of seeds.

THE LAST HARVEST

Depending on your hardiness zone, it may also be time to harvest your herbs for drying or freezing.

When cutting herbs, remember to share some with your ladies—gather bunches to hang in the coop for nibbling and to leave a fresh scent. And dry some too. A sprinkling of mint or oregano in the nest boxes smells lovely and helps keep the ladies bug-free and healthy through the winter.

GARDEN CLEANUP TIME . . . OR IS IT?

Gardeners tend to fall into two rather passionate camps regarding the big fall cleanup. There is the Victorian-dominion-over-nature versus the let-nature-take-its-course approach. I'm with Gaia. Mother Nature knows what she's doing. I save my cleanup for spring.

Detractors of this laissez-faire style say cutting everything down to the ground and raking everything up is the best way to prevent diseases and pests from lurking all winter long. Leaving plant matter and dead leaves where they fall, however, means they act as natural mulch, and as they break down, their nutrients work back into the soil as nature planned. And instead of dead-heading and pruning everything, leaving flowering plants and grasses as they are for the cold season provides seeds for hungry wintering birds.

last bloom saloon

In northern zones, fall offers only a handful of late bloomers for the last of the foraging bees. So even if you don't love it, leave that volunteer goldenrod in the ground and blooming bright yellow until it goes to seed. Our dwindling populations of pollinators need it. I also have late-blooming asters and sunchokes in my garden—front and back—and you should see the bees just madly buzzing around the flowers in the golden fall sunlight.

BEE WISE BIRDS

I've observed my ladies for hundreds of hours and never seen one go after an insect that stings—not a bee, not a wasp. So keeping a hive of honeybees or setting up a solitary bee hotel or habitat is safe for your chickens and wonderful for your garden.

If you are adding a hive or trying to attract bees and other pollinators to your garden, please remember that it's imperative to garden organically and purchase only non-GMO plants and seeds. Some plant retailers are now including bee-friendliness information on the tags; if not, ask.

SIGNE LANGFORD PHOTO

They say hens are the Gateway Livestock. It's true. After hens, most folks start craving goats or bees or both. But if a proper hive of European honeybees isn't possible for you, creating a wild bee hotel is easy and satisfying.

grow your own pumpkin patch

If space permits in your late-spring garden, build a mound and plant a pumpkin or two. I grow pie pumpkins for the rambling vines and lovely big blossoms. The bees and other pollinators go nuts for them, and they're good eats too.

With a city full of hungry raccoons, I had to be happy with the blossoms I got from MY pie pumpkin vines. An actual pumpkin was not in the cards. But the blossoms are beautiful, stuffed with seasoned ricotta, fried or baked.

JACK-O'-LANTERN LEFTOVERS FOR THE LADIES

If you carve a pumpkin for Halloween and don't care to roast the seeds, scoop them out along with all that stringy stuff for your ladies. They love it all, and pumpkin seeds and flesh contain medicinal chemicals that can help treat bladder irritation, kidney infections and intestinal worms. Cucurbitacin is a compound found not only in pumpkin seeds, but in all of the Cucurbitaceae family—including cucumbers, gourds, melons and zucchini—and has been shown to demonstrate anti-parasitic activity in the lab setting. I buy two pumpkins in October, one for me and one for the ladies—that way, I don't have to share my seeds.

THE AUTUMN OF HER DAYS

"How long do chickens live?" It's a question I hear all the time. Another is "What do you do with your hens when they stop laying?" All good questions . . . without a one-size-fits-all answer. I've heard that a perfectly healthy chicken in an ideal situation can live to twelve years, give or take. From what I've seen with my own girls and others, four to six seems to be more like it.

My two ex-bats lived to the ripe old age of seven, almost eight, and that was a real feat for a couple of factory girls. On the other hand, I've had hens that seemed just fine at bedtime and were dead on the floor the next morning. You just never know. Especially when adopting rescues who have been through some very tough times.

As for how long they will lay, well, that also depends. Once hens start laying, they will most likely have about two or three very productive years. After that, egg laying can become sporadic—she'll take breaks, and those breaks will get longer and more frequent until she's in full-blown *henopause*.

Serious homesteaders or folks in the egg business will cull "spent" hens for the soup pot, but sentimental fools like me let them enjoy their retirement. Besides, they still perform all the other garden duties hens specialize at—bug eating, fertilizing, aerating—and I've observed that often once egg laying has stopped, the hen won't be too long for this world.

If you fall somewhere in the middle of the sentimentality meter, you might choose to take your old girls to a farm sanctuary (along with

a generous financial donation) so that you can replace them with fresh young things ready to give you another few years of eggs. Ask at the sanctuary if they have any spring chickens to trade!

COCK-A-DOODLE-DON'T!

For urban and suburban hen-keepers, adding a rooster to the flock is a big noisy no-no. Yes, the ladies quite like to have a man around, but I'm not so sure your neighbours would feel the same. "But," you ask, "don't you need a rooster to get eggs?" No. Ahem; calling all pre-menopausal ladies! Do you ovulate even without a man around the house? You do? Right, then. A hen will ovulate—produce an egg—with or without the prospect of it being fertilized, just like women do.

If you live in the country, go ahead and add a roo to the flock. He'll be a great protector of the gals, an early warning system for predators and, well, he'll keep the ladies *entertained*. And as long as the eggs are collected every day and a fertilized egg doesn't get set on by a hen—which would cause it to develop an embryo—it's fine.

I think hens do enjoy having a rooster around; it probably feels right to them. But just like most of nature, a flock of hens hates a vacuum, so often a top or mature hen will take on the role of rooster. She'll be more dominant: she might even mount the other hens, do the rooster dance, dote on and share delicious tidbits with a favoured hen, even squawk out a tragic cock-a-doodle-doo now and then. But not to worry—it's only the secondary sexual characteristics that make the switch; she won't be able to fertilize an egg.

OPPOSITE, CLOCKWISE FROM TOP LEFT: mystery mushroom (SL); ripening wild grapes (DG); hens are funny by nature (SL).

ginger, the gender-bender

It's not terribly common, but hens can and do turn into roosters . . . sort of. The bits inside don't change, but the comb and wattles may grow and the feathers come in longer and flashier, especially the classic, showy rooster tail and elegant hackles. This happened with my old girl Ginger. At about age seven, she had stopped laying, then went through a complete moult, and when her feathers came back, presto change-o, she looked like a rooster. She took a best girl, Nelly—and man oh man could she make mincemeat of a squirrel if it annoyed her flock!

BEFORE

AFTER

SIGNE LANGFORD PHOTOS

In her last year of life, Ginger embarked on an amazing journey from hen to rooster-*ish*. She had stopped laying (*henopause*), had a complete moult, and when her feathers came back, they came back with rooster characteristics. Notice the long, showy tail and hackles.

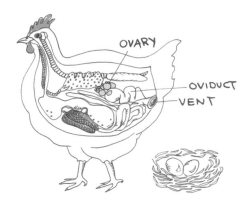

Labels on illustration: OVARY, OVIDUCT, VENT

A CHICKEN IN THE OVEN AND OTHER SCENES OF DIY CHICKEN DOCTORING

On a farm, when valuable livestock—a prize bull or show hen—falls ill, the vet is called in. But when one of a dozen or a hundred laying hens shows signs of sickness, it's generally curtains. This chicken will be removed from the rest of the flock to avoid infecting the other birds, watched and put on a general antibiotic. Or it will be culled (euthanized) or just left to die. Practical? Yes. Nice? No. And if you keep only a few hens, all with super-cute names and all of which you're wildly in love with, practicality and fiscal prudence can start taking a back seat to sentimentality.

But chickens get sick and injured. After laying eggs and generally being awesome, it's what they do best. They eat stuff they shouldn't. They get into scraps with each other; get preyed upon (bitten, gashed, generally roughed up); suffer egg-binding; have bum, crop and lady-part problems; and are susceptible to a whole host of poultry diseases. I'm not telling you this to make you panic or turn tail on the idea of getting hens; my point is that you either have very deep pockets and don't mind dropping a small fortune on veterinary care *or* you prepare yourself for a fair bit of home country doctorin'.

In almost 10 years of hen-keeping I've made only one trip to my avian vet with an injured

there's one in every flock: the vent-pecker

Some hens turn out to be vent-peckers. Lizzy Borden was one. She'd sneak up on the dog or one of her flock mates and let them have it, right on the bull's eye, as it were. Is a bum-pecker just being a jerk? Who knows? But it was important to keep an eye on her victims for signs of real injury; once she drew blood, she would become obsessed with pecking at it and this could spiral out of control.

On the other hand, don't be surprised to see a hen gobble up one of her own or her coop mate's fallen feathers. It's protein after all, and nature doesn't often let perfectly good nourishment go to waste.

bird. Ginger, one of my original flock, had somehow torn her comb away from her scalp and was bleeding—not a little bit, you understand, but slasher-movie style—all over herself and me. I tried wrapping her head up, but with only one set of hands and a wriggling bird, it proved impossible. I tried dusting the wound with blood-stop powder, but as soon as it started working, Ginger would give her head a shake and dislodge the clot . . . and we'd be right back to square one. At first, I tried to take a hard line and just let nature take its course, but truth was I would have felt like a monster if I'd just let her slowly bleed to death, so I bundled her up and off to the clinic we went. A hundred and change later, she came home good as new in a spiffy blue turban, and I was super-relieved. On that occasion, spending the money on professional care was the right thing to do *for me*. Every other time I've been faced with an injury or illness, I've dealt with it on my own the best I could, or called friends for a helping hand.

While there may have been some hens that could have been saved by a vet, often when a particular problem occurs once, it will recur. And so the sick-bird-spend-a-fortune-to-get-better-only-to-get-sick-again cycle begins, so again it is realistic to be self-sufficient when it comes to caring for your hens.

Hen-keeper Karen Bertelsen acknowledges too that part of keeping hens is losing them. They're pets, but they do often leave us much sooner than we expect, "some even sooner than a goldfish being taken care of by a five-year-old." But for the time that her lucky ladies are with her, she spoils them and they spoil her with incredible eggs. "I too have been learning on the job. And, yes, I will admit with some remorse that I did not save every hen that might have been saved if I'd rushed it in the middle of the night to the emergency vet. But again it comes down to the cost of veterinarian care and that mental shift we make as hen-keepers who treat our birds as something between pets and livestock."

As a hen-keeper, I believe it's not only vital to learn to diagnose and be willing to treat the most common ailments, it's my *responsibility*. Learn to recognize the first signs of trouble and give your hens the best treatment you can. Keep them warm, comfortable and under observation. I bring my hens inside the house when they need treatment; it's the easiest way to keep a close watch on them and keep them warm, which I do by setting up a "hospital" box on the opened oven door or in front of the toasty glass-enclosed fireplace. Extra sleep is just as healing for hens as it is for us when we're feeling unwell. So keep the hospital box dark, covered with a blanket or towel.

Much of what you know about your hens is learned through touch. It's important to have

SIGNE LANGFORD PHOTO

this sort of sensory intelligence, so that you can use your hands to detect illness. Hold and handle every part of your girls, even if they squawk and fuss. Learn what their abdomen feels like when perfectly healthy so you'll be able to tell if it ever feels off: hot, hard, ridged, inflamed or bloated. Get used to their normal temperature. Hold their feet to become familiar with what a healthy foot feels like.

Your ladies shouldn't smell bad in any way. When holding them, appreciate their birdy smell—a lovely, soft perfume of straw, feathers, grain. If there are any sour, poopy, rotten or just plain icky odours emitting from anywhere, this is likely a sign of infection, illness, or at the very least, a dirty girl that needs a spa day (see Girls' Spa Day, page 85)!

Here's a list of some of the conditions I've encountered and treated, successfully or not. Ultimately, the first step in keeping your flock happy and healthy is watching them—truly

Virgina creeper turns a beautiful red in autumn but the berries are poisonous to man and beast!

observing each hen—to note how they sit, walk, perch, behave, sleep, eat and poop when well. While they can't tell you when they're ill, body language can speak volumes. And for every diagnosis I've had to make or procedure I've done on my hens, I've found a helpful how-to video on the web.

Bumblefoot

This is an abscess in the sole of the foot. I noticed Miss Vicky limping one morning, so had a look, and sure enough, there was a small, smooth black spot: the beginnings of bumblefoot. I wrapped her in a towel, cleaned the area, and with very sharp disinfected tweezers dug out the kernel or spot, along with all of the surrounding dead tissue. I filled the wound with antibiotic ointment and sent her on her merry way. And yes, we made it through the whole procedure *sans* anaesthetic. A hen's foot is very tough—she barely even flinched—and anyway, anaesthetics are best left to the pros.

Calcium Deficiency

It's another girl thing. From time to time, your ladies may be short on calcium due to diet, lack of

Watermelon sprinkled with calcium powder is a great hot weather snack with a healthy kick.

vitamins, too little sunshine, illness or parasites. But it's easy to top it up. Add liquid calcium to their water or powdered calcium to a favourite wet treat—I sprinkle ground calcium tablets or powdered eggshells onto watermelon slices or mix it into oatmeal or polenta (see Back from Whence It Came, page 124).

Dropped Yolk or Peritonitis

I've always thought that bit between a woman's ovary and the opening of the fallopian tube was poorly designed. First of all, why the heck doesn't the ovary have a little door—you know, like a sphincter muscle to let the egg out? Why must it explode month after month? And why does the hapless little egg have to make that terrifying floating leap from ovary to the mouth of the fallopian tube? When an egg fails to make that leap and there just happens to be a feisty little sperm way the heck up there, an ectopic pregnancy can occur. That's a pregnancy outside the womb, in the abdominal cavity.

Well, a hen's internal set-up is fairly similar. All her ova or yolks dangle precariously, like a cluster of golden grapes, at the opening of her oviduct (a fallopian tube–like pipe). That yolk has to float in the right direction too, and if it doesn't make it, can drop down into the abdomen to cause a horrible, often deadly infection. It's a common ailment, and failing emergency surgery, one that will most often mean the end of a hen. I've treated dropped yolk with antibiotics, and that's helped see a hen through the most acute phase of it, hopefully easing some pain and taking down any fever, but ultimately, the symptoms come back once she's off the antibiotics. Some hen-keepers will simply euthanize a hen when dropped yolk is suspected. In rare instances, the dropped yolk will be absorbed and cleaned up by the body, but more often than not it is unhealthy and tainted with bacteria that will kill the hen; this is septic egg yolk peritonitis and once the hen is showing signs of illness it's usually fatal. This is another instance where mapping out your hens' bodies with your hands will really come in, um, handy. Feel her normal healthy abdomen so you'll know when it feels different. With this ailment, it will be hot, inflamed, spongy and bloated, and she might even be pooping yolk.

Egg Binding and Vent Prolapse

You might notice your hen has not laid in a couple of days, is staying inside her nest too long, is off her food, walking funny, sitting too much, looking droopy with a downward-pointing tail and is just not herself. If this is the case, she might be suffering from an egg that got stuck somewhere on its journey out. Her muscles might be too weak to work it out or the shell too soft or the egg too big—there are a number of reasons for binding. What you need to do is help her get that egg in motion, and that means it's time to don your hen gynecologist cap—and gloves if you like, although I don't bother with gloves as it's crucial to be able to feel textures and perform a very delicate procedure.

First, draw a deep hot bath and get her soaking. Line the bottom of the sink or bin with a rubber dishwashing mat first so she's got something to grip onto. While she's in the water, gently massage her abdomen; you're checking with your hands to feel where the egg is and relaxing her clenched muscles or painful tummy. If you find it—an egg will feel like a hard lump—gently massage it toward her vent. You may be up to your elbows in water for a good long while, so get comfortable. Occasionally, a warm soak and massage is all it takes for her to pass the egg. Other

COCK OF THE WALK

times I've had to go in. *All the way in.* And, yes, with no gloves. But please, before you try this at home do plenty of homework: read, watch how-to videos or find an old hand (as it were) to show you how it's done.

Vent prolapse is when the inside of the vent is partially expelled due to muscle weakness, from passing an overly large egg or just from a combination of age, gravity and the day-in-day-out strain of laying. Most cases are easy to spot—a pink, fleshy bulge where a dainty and demure vent once was!

Turn the hen upside down and, with a good dollop of hemorrhoid cream or petroleum-based antibiotic ointment, gently push the vent back inside. Keep her upside down for a few moments to let gravity help, while gently massaging everything back into its proper place, then top up her calcium intake by adding some crushed eggshells to her food (see Eggshells Are All They're Cracked Up to Be, page 124). This happened to my rescued Silkie, Cindy Loo—it was most unsettling to see, but very quickly remedied, never to happen again. Whew!

Flystrike

After Ginger died, my friend Montana Jones, a sheep farmer and magnificently principled she-wolf and protector of heritage species, said to me, "Well, it's official. You've dealt with the worst thing there is—if you can handle flystrike, you can handle anything." Ginger died when she was pushing seven; that's about four years more than most ex-bats live, but she was so lovely and one of my first girls, so I wanted her to go on forever.

First, she developed a systemic infection, most likely from a dropped yolk, which I semi-successfully treated with antibiotics, but she was slowing down, sleeping more and eating less, and the infection came back with a vengeance. Once again, I began administering antibiotics but this time she didn't rally. On the third day of her steady decline I picked her up for a cuddle and noticed a horrible rotting smell, but couldn't tell where it was coming from—inside or out. I set her down on a lawn chair in the sun by the kitchen door, and two things happened: one lovely and one horrific.

As she lay there, eyes closed, listing to one side, the rest of her flock gathered around her. They didn't pick on her, they didn't fuss, they just each did their own thing—preening, napping, sun bathing—but all within inches of her. It was clear to me that they knew something was up, and if their matriarch couldn't be with them as they puttered around the garden, they were going to stand by her.

And then the horrid thing happened. As Ginger shifted, I saw something glisten or did it move? I looked closer. It took a second or two for my brain to interpret what my eyes were conveying; yes, something was moving . . . wait . . . *what the!* A writhing cluster of tiny greyish maggots was feasting on Ginger's flesh. It was seriously horrifying.

I ran upstairs to the computer. "Maggots on dying chicken—please help," I clicked, and read

as fast as my eyes and brain could absorb the information: *Bathe in salt water. Clean away all maggots and dead tissue. Disinfect, slather with antibiotic cream.* I supported Ginger in hot salty water with one hand, and with the other frantically washed the maggoty wound, flushing the water against it and brushing at it with my fingers. I rinsed and rinsed, but as I drained the sink, preparing for a refill, she gave a shudder and died right then in my arms. I had discovered the flystrike too late to prevent the local infection from going systemic. Are you still with me? I hope so, because even though you will have to deal with a few unpleasant things—maybe even flystrike, heaven forbid—having chickens is still so worth any of the gore I've encountered along the way.

Ingrown Feathers

Like an ingrown hair on us, this is a feather that zigged when it should have zagged. Instead of heading straight out, it grows horizontally under the skin, causing inflammation, irritation, infection or worse if it goes undetected. But it's easy to fix: start with a hot salty bath, then disinfect the area, open the skin with a scalpel or sharp-ended pair of tweezers and pluck it out. If there's bleeding, use blood-stop powder. Finish with a drop

the trouble with iodine

I prefer alcohol-based hand sanitizer over iodine to disinfect wounds. Why? Because iodine stains red, and when a hen "sees red," she simply *must* peck at it. You put a hen out into the flock with a red spot on her and you may as well put the poor girl on the menu. That's why it's also vital to wipe away any blood from an injury or plucked feather. Have I mentioned that hens are really just small, adorable, bloodthirsty dinosaurs?

of hand sanitizer and a bit of antibiotic cream. Done!

Intestinal Worms

This is another almost unavoidable pest, but very treatable. Through normal hunting and pecking, a hen may ingest parasitic worm eggs. The eggs hatch and grow into worms—most often intestinal. You can tell if your ladies have worms by periodically inspecting poop. If you see what looks like tiny white grains of rice, those are worm eggs. Sometimes you'll see segments of adults or even whole live or dead adults in poop. There are both natural and chemical treatments, but since worms can become a problem rather quickly, causing anemia and robbing your ladies of their nourishment, I tend to treat them with a strong pharmaceutical dewormer. Just don't eat your ladies' eggs for a minimum of two weeks after a dose, or more if instructed by the package. Chuck them into the compost or—and I talk about this polarizing practice in Back from Whence it Came, page 124—let your ladies eat them.

Mites, Lice and Scaly Leg Mite Infestation

Just like fleas on our beloved dogs and cats, and microscopic mites on us, hens attract miniscule creepy crawlers that live on them to suck their blood or eat dead skin and feather debris—what I call bird dust. A hen-keeper's goal is to keep the situation under control. I'm doubtful they can ever be 100 percent eliminated but, obviously, the fewer the better. Mite and lice control comes down to coop and bird hygiene, preventative sprays and powders, and natural controls such as the somewhat controversial neem oil and diatomaceous earth, both of which have fans and detractors.

Mites like places to hide, so pay special attention to cracks, crevices and straw for mites and

Lovely Millie was a hodgepodge of breeds who laid eggs too big for her own good. Ultimately it's what ended her life too soon.

their eggs. When inspecting and treating your ladies, check obsessively—seriously, I'll be in there several times a day—during the acute phase of an outbreak. As the treatments take effect, narrow inspections down to once daily, then weekly, and pay special attention to the vent area and base of the tail, where the little devils like to hang out. That's also where you're most likely to find feather shafts encrusted with lice eggs and possibly patches of reddened, irritated skin. An internet search for "how to treat chicken mites" will show you everything you need to know.

Sour or Impacted Crop

Found at the base of the neck, the crop is the part of the oesophagus where food digestion starts. To keep on top of crop troubles, learn what it feels like when empty and when full of food. A sour or impacted crop will feel like a water balloon and you might be able to detect a hard lump or blockage. And your hen's breath may smell of beer or yeasty fermentation—that's right, I'm saying you should become acquainted with healthy hen breath too!

I noticed Millie, a cuckoo Old English Game bantam mystery cross, looking too quiet and sleepy, so gave her the once-over. Sure enough, her crop was bloated and spongy with a hard lump. I wrapped her up in a tea towel, turned her upside down until she was almost vertical and started massaging her crop. Out poured a lot of nasty, fermented liquid and gunk, but the lump remained. Some chicken sites on the internet recommend cutting the crop open and pulling the blockage out—without anaesthetic—but I'm just not up for that, so I took the slower route, giving her butter, olive oil, yogurt and massage. And within a day, the lump softened enough to pass from her crop to her gizzard and Millie was well again. Until the next time. Are you sensing a pattern here? Like I said earlier, chickens are creatures of habit and, sadly, that extends to health issues too.

Chicken First Aid Kit
- All-natural olive-oil non-stick cooking spray
- Antibiotic ointments, human or veterinarian; petroleum-based is best as it's waterproof
- Blood-stop (styptic) powder
- Calcium: liquid, powder or tablets
- Deworming medication
- Dog nail clippers
- Epsom or sea salt
- Eye droppers
- Flashlight (small but bright)
- Gauze bandages
- Hemorrhoid cream: petroleum-based
- Needle and thread
- Petroleum jelly
- Popsicle sticks or wooden tongue depressors for splints
- Powdered veterinarian electrolytes/vitamins
- Rubbing alcohol or hand sanitizer
- Scalpels
- Self-sticking wound tape
- Syringes
- Toothbrush
- Tweezers

HEN THERAPY
At Cobble Hills Farm Sanctuary near Stratford, Ontario, hens arrive by the truckload—in pet carriers, crates and cages—and there's nothing pretty about it.

In late fall and early winter, battery cage egg factories empty massive sheds—the average barn holds about 20,000 "spent" hens. These pitiful

 have you hugged your chicken today?

They may not love it, may squawk a little and wiggle and fuss, but daily holding and petting is very important for the health of your relationship . . . with the hens, that is! At some point in their lives, you are going to have to handle them—bathe, bandage or medicate—and if they're not used to it, catching and holding onto them is going to be ridiculously difficult and scratchy! So gently hold each of your ladies as often as you can, stroking her under the chin and giving her a light little scratch all around the skin parts of her face. Don't try to chase and catch a hen that's never been held lovingly before; it will only terrify her. Wait until nightfall when the hen has tucked herself in to gently approach her.

These factory hens were rescued between the cages they lived in and the slaughterhouse they were headed to. Depleted, bald and starved for sunlight, soil and mental stimulation, with time, these ladies came back to life and grew beautiful again.

birds are so exhausted, so depleted from forced intensive egg-laying, that they've often lost the ability to produce feathers and are as bald as any bird in your grocer's meat case. Author and adoption advocate—of both hens and humans—Christen Doidge Shepherd thinks these sorry-looking gals are beautiful and deserve a second chance.

Christen has taken up to 100 hens at a time. Often the egg producers are willing to sell her the birds for a couple of dollars each; after all, they're destined for the landfill or a massive composter, or the slaughterhouse where they'll be made into chicken dogs and soup.

Initially frightened and blinded by natural sunshine—something they've never seen in their short lives of 12 to 18 months—these hens will be able to stretch their wings, feel solid ground under their feet, hunt and peck, lay in straw-lined nesting boxes and roost at bedtime.

It was soon after Christen had purchased a farm—a dream of hers since age 10—that she heard about the plight of laying hens. Christen

is not the sort to turn a blind eye to suffering: "They've been abused, had a really rough life, but given a chance, they can heal. I thought it mirrored the story of abused kids perfectly." So, Christen, a mom to six kids—two grown biological sons and four adopted siblings—embarked on a labour of love. "I invited kids from two nearby group homes to work with the hens, to take care of them, to help them heal."

Each of the kids picked a hen to call their own, with the first order of business being nail trimming. "Their toes have been painfully wrapped around wire mesh their whole lives, so their nails grow too long." Shepherd's big blue eyes light up when she talks about her kids and her hens: "It's incredible to see the gentleness these boys show to the hens; to see them so gently handling their hens and giving them pedicures. It's just lovely."

These are kids who have suffered every manner of abuse and neglect. They'd been written off and were being warehoused, thought incapable of empathy or attachments. What no one counted

One of Christen Doidge Shepherd's kids, Samantha, with Wonky Wing, a plucky rescued hen wearing a nifty little vest to keep her warm until her feathers grow back in.

 ## the ugly truth about battery cages

The egg is a perfect, versatile, indispensable food, an important part of most of the world's cuisines. But pity the poor hen that hatches into a life of caged slavery, only to be discarded a year or two later. In a debate with a representative of Big Egg, sustainable American farmer Joel Salatin—my hero and a passionate advocate of raising happy hens—said, "If one in three households in the US kept even a few laying hens, we wouldn't need industrial egg factories."

Imagine six to eight hens crammed into a cold, hard wire cage the size of a typical microwave oven. Now imagine tiers and tiers of these cages, row on row, in massive sheds; bright, unnatural light glaring down for fourteen hours a day, with no room to move, stretch or be a hen. Imagine the skin- and lung-burning ammonia of feces. Now imagine this in the millions and you've imagined where most eggs come from. Battery cage operations are also Petri dishes for viruses—such a large quantity of stressed and unhealthy bodies in one place provides viruses and bacteria with the perfect place to strut their deadly stuff and mutate at lightning speed.

And if we can keep a few hens, we can rescue a few ex-bats and undo some of the suffering and injustice—and we can feed ourselves and our families beautiful, whole, delicious food in the process.

on, not even Christen, was the degree to which these kids would identify and bond with the hens.

"People think these kids are lost, but they're not. They just need a chance to show how good they really are."

With time together, the hens and the kids learn to trust each other, and while the hens grow silky new feathers, the kids develop self-esteem and a sense of accomplishment. Holding a softly clucking, trusting hen is soothing; kids labelled as aggressive or incapable of connecting, open up. Christen just glows when she reminisces about seeing completely disconnected kids sustain eye contact—a first for them!—with the hens.

When the hens have healed, they are adopted out to forever homes, and the cycle can begin all over again with a new batch of rescues—hen and human.

the egg: autumn recipes

There's something about the fall—even more than winter—that brings the fleeting nature of the seasons into sharp focus. The garden has peaked: any fruit the ladies, garden critters or I didn't get to litters the ground. Leaves are withering, the sugars rushing back down to the roots; seeds are forming; squirrels are stashing and bees are gorging. Almost everything that's happening out there now is in an effort to guarantee a return in the spring. I can't help but be swept up in the prevailing survivalist mood and it's in the kitchen that it shows the most. I fantasize about the perfect root cellar, and if I hadn't been born with some serious impulse control, there'd be an endless supply of cakes and cookies. The kitchen is where I want to be, soothing my sadness with soups. And yes, sadness, because I won't get to spend as much time with the ladies as I do in the summer, and because I wish they didn't have to endure another winter. But, like I said, there will be soups to make, bread to bake and jelly to put into jars, and in September, a birthday cake for me which I will share with the girls—they need a little cold-weather insulation after all!

Everyone deserves a little celebration now and then. Just remember, no chocolate cake for the ladies! Chocolate is toxic to most critters, including chickens.

breakfast stromboli

SERVES 6

I'm not a fussbudget about pizza dough; if you want to make it from scratch, be my guest. If not, do what I often do: grab a ball of ready-made from the bakery. It's the stuff inside that makes or breaks this dish, and breakfast shouldn't be too hard on a sleepyhead. Likewise, unless you insist on making your own pesto, use your favourite store-bought brand.

7 free-run eggs, divided
Sea salt and freshly ground pepper to taste
1 cup (250 mL) coarsely chopped slab
    bacon or ham
Flour for dusting
Dough for 1 pizza, at room temperature
¼ cup (60 mL) basil pesto, or to taste
4 oz (110 g) brie, sliced or coarsely chopped,
    or to taste
1 cup (250 mL) coarsely chopped and drained
    tomato (about 1 large)
1 tsp (5 mL) extra-virgin olive oil

01. Preheat oven to 375f (190c) and line a baking sheet with parchment paper; set aside.
02. Break 6 of the eggs into a medium bowl, season with salt and pepper, and whisk until fully blended; set aside.
03. In a skillet over medium-high heat, fry bacon until crisp. Drain off some of the fat if there's a lot, turn heat down to low and return skillet to heat. Add the eggs from the bowl, mix with the bacon and cook for about 3 minutes, or until set but not dry; remove from heat and set aside.
04. Lightly dust the counter and rolling pin with flour and roll out pizza dough into a rectangle of about 10 × 14 inches (25 × 36 cm).
05. Spread the pesto over one half of the pizza, right up to about 2 inches (5 cm) from the edges.
06. Evenly distribute the slices of brie on top of the pesto, then evenly distribute the eggs and bacon on top of the brie. Sprinkle the chopped tomato evenly over the eggs.
07. In a small bowl or cup, use a fork to beat the remaining egg with the olive oil. Using a pastry brush, brush the edges of the empty side of the pizza dough and fold over the filling; press down and pinch to make a nice, tight seal. At this point, you can either leave the dough in a half-moon shape and transfer directly to the baking sheet, or roll into a log and place on the baking sheet with the seam side down.
08. Brush the rest of the egg-and-oil wash over the top and sides of the stromboli. Use a sharp-tipped knife to slash a few steam vents. Bake for about 25 minutes or until golden and bubbly with deliciousness oozing from the vents, which is how I think the dish got its name. It must have reminded the cook who invented it of the famous Stromboli volcano!
09. If you can stand it, allow the stromboli to rest for a few minutes before cutting into slices for serving; the interior is lava-hot!

tip

This recipe can easily be made
into minis or individual
pizza pockets for breakfast
on the go.

I own a large double-decker pot steamer, so that works great for me. Chinese bamboo steamers are also good; if you have one that's large enough to accommodate the bowl and small enough to fit inside a pot with a lid, you're in business!

If you don't have a wire rack or bamboo steamer, an overturned heat-proof dish can work as a sort of pedestal inside the wok or pot.

chef roger mooking's steamed eggs

SERVES 2

Chef Roger Mooking and Helen, my late ex-bat Leghorn, became fast friends when he visited my garden between running here and flying there. I think she could tell he's a fan of free-run eggs. Roger told me a story about his grandfather's ingenious coop.

"When my father was a very small boy, his family lived in a house on stilts on the southern tip of Trinidad. Protecting the house from floods was the initial purpose of this very common Caribbean architectural feature but my grandfather, Moses Mooking, being the ever-inventive, food-obsessed person that he was, saw that as prime poultry real estate. He very quickly caged the stilted area below the house with chicken wire and outfitted it with everything a bunch of chickens need to free-range and flourish. Although my father hated tending to his newly created chores, the entire family loved the fresh eggs and curry chicken on Sunday. This henhouse in Icacos is a part of Mooking family culinary legend."

2 tsp (10 mL) extra-virgin olive oil

4 free-run eggs

2 Tbsp (30 mL) finely diced crimini mushrooms

1 tsp (5 mL) finely diced green onion

2 Tbsp (30 mL) tomato sauce or passata
  (ready-made is fine)

Pinch of kosher salt

Few grindings of freshly ground black pepper

Leaves from 1 stem fresh tarragon

01. In a large, shallow pot, add enough water to reach about 1 inch (2.5 cm) in depth. Place a small wire rack inside the pot and bring the water to a boil. Reduce to a simmer and place lid on while preparing the eggs.

02. Place the olive oil in an earthenware or other heat-proof bowl, then crack in the eggs, making sure to keep yolks intact.

03. Evenly sprinkle mushrooms, green onion, dollops of tomato sauce, salt and pepper over top of the eggs. You can add the tarragon now—as I do—or just before serving. I like the look of it cooked.

04. Place the bowl on top of the wire rack inside the pot and cover the bowl with a fitted lid, then cover the pot. Allow to steam for 6 to 8 minutes, or until the whites have set. Carefully remove the hot bowl from the pot and place on a plate. Sprinkle tarragon leaves over the bowl if you haven't done so already.

05. Serve immediately with your choice of toast or flatbread.

Chef Roger Mooking and Helen became fast friends, despite Chef's fondness for spicy chicken wings.

SIGNE LANGFORD PHOTO

a scottish chef's scotch eggs

SERVES 4 AS AN APPETIZER OR 2 FOR LUNCH

Chef John Higgins, Director of the George Brown College Chef School, had humble culinary beginnings. "As a child growing up in Scotland, the diet was mince and tatties (meat and potatoes) most days and fish on Friday. My love affair with Scotch eggs started at my grannie's house. I thought she was a magician; an egg in meat all cooked and deep fried with a crisp exterior? *This was gourmet!* She served them with HP brown sauce or some piccalilli, but who cares? It tasted like nothing I had ever tasted. I guess you could say I lost my virginity to a Scotch egg." That would be Chef's culinary virginity, folks! Settle down!

"Since those early days, I have eaten my good share of Scotch eggs, and for the past 10 years I have made them at charity events in a host of different styles, from the classic to wrapped in black pudding, haggis or crabmeat. I've even made them vegetarian. But my favourite is the classic Scotch egg with Branston pickle on the side; it's to die for. You know, I had a good laugh recently, when I saw all the hipsters and their Scotch eggs in a Toronto magazine—made me wonder what came first: the chicken or the egg or the Scotch egg?"

Um, the Scotch egg, naturally. Didn't the Scots invent *everything?*

Neutral vegetable oil for deep frying

1 lb (455 g) raw heritage pork sausage meat (I'm a fan of Berkshire)

2 tsp (10 mL) Worcestershire sauce

1 tsp (5 mL) minced fresh thyme

1 tsp (5 mL) finely minced fresh flat-leaf parsley

Sea salt and freshly ground black pepper to taste, divided

2 free-run eggs

½ cup (120 mL) all-purpose flour

1½ cups (350 mL) fine, unseasoned dry bread crumbs

4 free-run eggs, hard-boiled and peeled (see Hard-Boiling: My Way, page 26)

01. Preheat oven to 350F (180C) and line a baking sheet with parchment paper; set aside.

02. Into a large bowl, add the sausage meat (if you've purchased sausages, squeeze the meat from the casings), Worcestershire sauce, thyme, parsley, salt and pepper; blend with super-clean hands until evenly combined.

03. In a small bowl, add raw eggs, salt and pepper and beat. Add the flour to a second small bowl, and the bread crumbs to a third small bowl, and line up in a row beside the beaten egg. You'll be dredging and coating, production line style, in a minute!

04. On a clean surface, divide the sausage meat into 4 balls. Flatten each ball into a disc large enough to fully wrap around the egg. Work the meat around each egg and make sure there are no gaps and the meat layer is fairly even.

continued on page 150

A young Miss Vicky when she first came to me from the SPCA.

SIGNE LANGFORD PHOTO

05. In a deep fryer or a deep saucepan over medium heat (with a lid kept nearby in case of fire), fill pan about two-thirds full with oil and heat oil to 375F (190C). Use a deep-fat thermometer for accurate cooking. If the oil is too cold, the result will be oily and sodden. If it's too hot, the outside will burn before the meat has properly cooked.

06. Dip the sausage-wrapped egg into the flour to coat very lightly. Roll in the beaten eggs, then roll in the bread crumbs. Now give it one more dip in the eggs, then back into the bread crumbs. Set aside on a plate and repeat with the remaining eggs. (I give any leftover bread crumbs to the ladies!)

07. Using a frying basket or slotted spoon, carefully lower the eggs into the hot oil one at a time and fry until golden brown, about 2 minutes. Carefully transfer each egg to the baking sheet and when they're all done, pop them into the oven and bake for 10 minutes.

08. To serve, cut each egg in half and serve with a little salad, a tasty chutney or relish—Branston pickle all the way!—some lovely Scottish potato bread and a strong Scottish ale.

blank slate crepe

MAKES 12 TO 15 CREPES

There were a few Montreal restaurants Father took me to as a kid. The best of all was La Crêpe Bretonne. The place dim and rustic with chunky wood and brick. Girls in hats and long Breton dresses. And with a huge griddle in the centre of the dining room where a cook poured, filled and folded massive crepes that were crispy at the edges and all folded up over whatever you'd asked for in the middle. I always got bacon and maple for dinner, then strawberries and vanilla ice cream for dessert. Father and I were in heaven—not even the head-shaking and disgusted glares coming from Mother perturbed us.

This is a basic neutral crepe recipe. You might want to add 1 teaspoon (5 mL) of vanilla extract to the batter if using sweet fillings, and you may add spice or finely chopped herbs or even super-finely chopped green onion to savoury crepes. It's very versatile.

2 free-run eggs
2 cups (475 mL) all-purpose flour
3 cups (710 mL) organic 3.5 percent milk
2 Tbsp (30 mL) melted butter or oil
Clarified butter, ghee or oil for the pan

01. Place first four ingredients into a tall jug and blend until perfectly smooth with an immersion blender. If you don't have one of those, a bowl with a whisk, stand mixer or electric beaters are just fine too.

02. Transfer the batter to a covered jug to rest in the fridge overnight—it cooks up better if the gluten has some time to develop. When ready to make the crepes, give the batter another stir, since it will separate a bit overnight.

03. Set a crepe pan over medium-high heat. Here's where you have some choice: what will you use to keep it from sticking? Adding butter each time will make them too oily and the butter tends to burn at the heat we need to get a nice surface on the crepe. You can use clarified butter, ghee or oil. They all work; it's just a matter of taste and efficiency.

04. Add your fat of choice to the hot pan to coat, then pour enough batter to thinly coat the bottom of the pan. You'll have to figure it out for yourself, but try about ¼ to ⅓ cup (60 to 80 mL) to start with.

05. Tilt the pan and swirl the batter around in the pan to coat. This takes a bit of practice, and there are specialized tools you can buy for this if you prefer. When the pan is coated, give it a shake every few seconds. When the crepe starts to come away from the pan (after about 2 minutes), it's ready to flip. Use a spatula or have fun perfecting the old in-the-air flip!

06. Let the other side cook for a couple of seconds—just enough to dry any liquid batter. Slide the crepe off the pan onto a plate. Continue with the rest of the batter, greasing the pan before each crepe. And don't worry, the first crepe is always a disaster.

07. Now you have a stack of crepes ready to be filled with whatever grabs you. Try Crème Anglaise (page 51) and jam, coconut egg jam (page 161), scrambled eggs and sausage, poached eggs and blanched asparagus with a lovely white wine or cheese sauce. You get the idea!

curried eggs with paneer

SERVES 4 TO 6

My high school sweetheart's mother was a terrifying, mean, upper-crusty Brit. I didn't like her, she didn't like me, and that was that. The fact that I was dating her son made me wicked. Being a vegetarian made me wicked *and* weird. He and I dated for about six months—an eternity when you're 15—and in that time I was invited to dinner exactly once. The mother made a chicken curry for everyone. For me, she scooped some of the sauce over hard-boiled eggs, proclaiming out loud, "Look Siggy, these are for you! I thought it was awfully clever of me!" I thought it was horrible—rubbery, sulphurous, overcooked eggs plopped into an incongruous sauce, given no time to marry.

The rest of that miserable night only comes back in bits: me chasing whole, slithering eggs around a plate, finally snaring one and just about gagging on the dry-as-dust yolk, and her administering Twenty Questions about My Future, which made swallowing the meal even harder.

I've taken this opportunity to rehabilitate my feelings about curried eggs. As for *the mother,* some feelings are beyond rehabilitation.

6 free-run eggs
3 cloves garlic, peeled
2-inch (5-cm) piece fresh ginger, peeled
1–2 hot fresh chili peppers
2 Tbsp (30 mL) fresh lemon juice
1 small red onion, thinly sliced, divided
¼ cup (60 mL) fresh cilantro,
     plus extra for garnish
3 Tbsp (45 mL) vegetable oil or ghee

8 oz (225 g) paneer, diced into 1-inch
     (2.5-cm) pieces
1 tsp (5 mL) garam masala
1 tsp (5 mL) turmeric powder
2 tsp (10 mL) black or yellow mustard seeds
2 tsp (10 mL) cumin seeds
½ tsp (2.5 mL) sea salt
2 medium tomatoes, coarsely chopped
¾ cup (180 mL) chicken or vegetable broth

01. Parboil the eggs: place eggs in a saucepan and cover with cold water. Set on high heat and bring to a boil. Boil for about 3 to 5 minutes, or just until the whites have set enough to peel and still hold together. Transfer eggs to a bowl of cold water. When cool enough to handle, very gingerly peel them and set aside.

02. In a food processor or very powerful blender, add the garlic, ginger, chili, lemon juice, cilantro and half of the onion slices, and blend until puréed; set aside. Do not lift the lid on this concoction with your nose directly over; you will sear your sinuses!

03. In a large heavy-bottomed skillet over medium heat, add oil or ghee and cubes of paneer. Cook until golden on both sides, about 5 minutes. Transfer paneer to a dish and set aside.

04. Add the remaining onion slices to the pan and cook for about 10 minutes or until golden, stirring often.

05. Add the aromatic purée to the pan of onions, and continue to cook until it also starts to turn golden, about 10 minutes. Stir often to prevent sticking and burning.

06. Add the dry spices and salt and fry for a minute more, stirring.

07. Add the tomatoes and cook until most of the liquid has cooked off and the sauce starts to dry out a bit. Keep stirring or it will stick and burn!

08. Add the paneer and peeled parboiled eggs, and very gently stir around to coat with the sauce. Add the broth, reduce heat and simmer for another 5 to 7 minutes to reduce the sauce just a titch and heat the eggs through.

09. To serve, spoon a couple of eggs and some sauce over rice or serve with bread—naan or a rustic white loaf. A side of yogurt is nice, and a handful of fresh cilantro leaves on top. It's also a good idea to pre-cut a little slash into each egg, so the diner doesn't have to chase it around the plate as I did on that night that shall live on in infamy.

Seriously, I was a delightful teenager—so why didn't my boyfriend's mother like me?

tip

The whole cilantro plant is usable and delicious. Most often we see just the leaves and most tender stems used, but the roots—once well washed of all grit—are super-flavourful and add so much to a vegetable stock or Thai-style soup.

tip

For this recipe, it's easier to make the won tons if you use small or peewee eggs. Perfect reason to adopt a bantam hen, if you ask me!

egg yolk won ton soup

SERVES 2

I love won ton soup and I love egg drop soup, so I thought I'd try putting them in the same bowl. It worked! The won tons are gorgeous and the marigold orange of my ladies' yolks glows through the wrappers.

3 cups (710 mL) organic chicken or vegetable broth

1 tsp (5 mL) soy sauce

2 tsp (10 mL) unseasoned rice wine vinegar

¼ tsp (1 mL) ground white pepper, or more to taste

2-inch (5-cm) piece fresh ginger, peeled and very finely julienned or minced

2 scallions, trimmed and finely sliced on the bias, white and green parts separated

A few sprigs fresh cilantro, finely minced, plus extra for garnish

12 won ton wrappers

6 whole cilantro leaves

6 free-run egg yolks, each in a separate dish

1 tsp (5 mL) sriracha sauce, or to taste

1 cup (250 mL) napa cabbage leaves, thinly sliced or chiffonade

¼ tsp (1 mL) toasted sesame oil

01. In a medium saucepan over medium heat, add the broth, soy sauce, vinegar, pepper, ginger, white parts of the scallions and minced cilantro; bring to a simmer. Reduce heat to very low—just to keep hot—and cover.

02. Set yourself up with the open package of won ton wrappers, a plate and a little dish of water for dipping your finger into when gluing the won ton wrappers shut.

03. Now, working with one won ton at a time, use your finger to wipe a bit of water around all four edges of the wrapper. Don't miss any spots; you need to create a perfectly tight seal. Place one perfect cilantro leaf in the centre of the wonton wrapper, then slide a yolk *gently* onto the leaf in the centre of the wonton wrapper. On the yolk, squeeze a tiny drop of sriracha or another favourite Asian chili sauce, then lay another won ton wrapper on top and press the edges together. Make sure it's well sealed, with no gaps where water can seep in and bust open your little bundles of joy. Repeat these steps with all 6 yolks, then set aside on a plate until ready to add to the soup.

04. Increase heat under the soup pot to medium, and bring back up to that sweet spot between a vigorous simmer and a low, gentle boil. Add the cabbage and green parts of the scallion. Stir and add the won tons while the soup is still moving around.

05. Try to keep the won tons from sticking to the bottom of the pot; if this happens, you risk overcooking the yolk or tearing the wrapper and losing the yolk, and I can assure you—from experience—that both outcomes will find you over-salting the soup with your bitter tears!

06. Keep the soup moving around very gently while the won tons cook, about 1½ to 2 minutes for a runny yolk. Add a few drops of sesame oil and serve immediately! Garnish with more fresh cilantro leaves if desired and offer more sriracha if you like it hot!

tip

These cakes are low-fat by nature, so try to eat them up on baking day! But if you have leftovers and they've become dry and rubbery, I like to use them in a dessert bread pudding, trifle, tiramisu or any other composed dessert that calls for cake soaked in coffee or boozy goodness.

golden chinese egg cakes

MAKES 12 CAKES OR 24 MINIS

Six simple ingredients and three steps are all it takes to whip up a batch of golden-topped, light-as-air mini cakes. Once you know what you're doing with these very few but delicious ingredients, you'll be able to play around with confidence. As long as you don't mess with proportions of dry and liquid too much, you can't go terribly wrong; this is one of those baking recipes where using a kitchen scale is really the best way to go. This one's a bit like science!

4 free-run eggs
7 oz (200 g) / 1 cup (250 mL) sugar
⅛ tsp (0.6 mL) sea salt
6 oz (170 g) / 1⅓ cups (320 mL) all-purpose flour
1 tsp (5 mL) baking powder
2½ Tbsp (37 mL) neutral-flavoured oil: peanut, safflower, sunflower, grapeseed

01. Preheat oven to 350F (180C). Line a 12-cup muffin tin (or 24-cup mini-muffin tin) with paper liners or lightly grease and flour; set aside.

02. In the bowl of a stand mixer or a large bowl with electric beaters, whip the eggs, sugar and salt together until pale yellow, light and airy. Start on medium speed but quickly increase to medium-high until desired consistency is achieved.

03. Sift the flour and baking powder together and, using a rubber spatula, gently fold the dry ingredients into the egg and sugar mixture; incorporate completely. This isn't like a muffin recipe where a few lumps are okay. Stir and fold until it's smooth.

04. Add the oil and stir well (without being too vigorous) to combine.

05. Fill the tins to about ½ inch (1.25 cm) from the top and bake for about 20 minutes or until the tops are golden and just firm. If you take a listen, you should hear the cakes crackling; I think that must be what delicious sounds like!

06. Cool the cakes on a tray until they're not too hot to handle, then remove from the tins and let them cool on a wire rack.

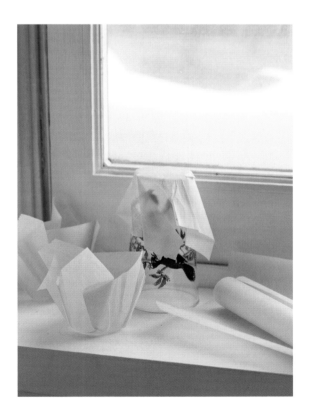

heartwarming savoury bread pudding

SERVES 6 TO 8

Bread pudding—or bread and butter pudding—is another custard-based dish that swings both ways: sweet or savoury. I think in North America we're most familiar with the sweet sort, but I truly love a tasty, cheesy, eggy savoury bread pudding. It's like a warm hug for your tummy. And, like so many of these basic, sort of tabula rasa recipes, once you've mastered the base, the world's your oyster. You can add all sorts—including oysters, come to think of it!

I made this dish for the lunch menu at Riverside Café, a restaurant I owned in the 1990s. At the restaurant I made individual puddings in ramekins, and you can do that too at home, but I prefer family style—in one big casserole dish—for group feasting. As for the cheeses I've called for, that's just my preference. If you can't find or don't like these cheeses, just use whatever cheese you like, but consider this: one cheese should add sharpness, one should provide melty goodness and one should add a soft, creamy surprise from bite to bite.

3 Tbsp (45 mL) butter, plus more for greasing the casserole

1 Tbsp (15 mL) olive oil

8 cups (2 L) coarsely chopped mixed mushrooms

¼ tsp (1 mL) + a pinch sea salt, divided

Freshly ground black pepper to taste, divided

1 shallot, finely chopped

1 clove garlic, finely chopped

8 cups (2 L) raw baby spinach

¼ cup (60 mL) medium-dry sherry

4 free-run eggs

1 cup (250 mL) 18 percent cream

½ cup (120 mL) 3.5 percent milk

1 Tbsp (15 mL) Dijon mustard

2 tsp (10 mL) finely chopped fresh thyme

¼ cup (60 mL) finely chopped fresh chives

Pinch freshly grated nutmeg

4 cups (1 L) cubed baguette or rustic country loaf

1 cup (250 mL) cherry or "cocktail" bocconcini

1 cup (250 mL) grated pecorino

1 cup (250 mL) grated old cheddar

01. Preheat oven to 375F (190C). Liberally butter a 9-inch (22.5-cm) oven-safe dish; set aside. Don't worry if the dish is a bit bigger or smaller; it'll still work.

02. Into a large skillet over medium-high heat, add butter and oil; once melted, add the mushrooms and stir often to prevent burning. Season with a pinch of salt and a couple of grinds of pepper. Cook for about 5 minutes, then add the chopped shallot and garlic.

03. After cooking for a further 10 minutes, add the spinach; stir and continue to fry until spinach wilts right down. Add the sherry and allow it to burn off. Keep frying until the pan is almost dry. Remove from heat and set aside to cool slightly.

04. In a very large bowl, whisk the eggs, cream, milk, mustard, thyme, chives, salt, pepper and nutmeg together until well blended. Add the bread cubes, bocconcini and the spinach and mushroom mixture; stir together and pour into the prepared casserole dish. Sprinkle the pecorino and cheddar evenly over top.

05. Cover the casserole with a lid or aluminum foil and bake for about 30 minutes. Remove lid and continue to bake for another 10 to 15 minutes. The bread pudding should rise a tiny bit; you'll know it's done when the top is golden and looks set with just a bit of wobble left.

06. Serve hot with a simple side salad and a dollop of Dijon. So cozy-good.

chef wing li's coconut egg jam

MAKES ABOUT 2½ CUPS (600 ML)

• •

The first time I tasted this sweet delight was at Linda Modern Thai restaurant in Toronto, and I was once again reminded of my idea that all restaurants should have "licking screens," for when something is so good, you wish you could lick the plate without horrifying onlookers.

Chef de Cuisine Wing Li from Linda Modern Thai shared his recipe. The only potentially hard-to-find ingredient called for is the pandan leaves. Pandan is also known as screw pine, and if you live near a major city you should be able to find it at a good Asian market.

1¼ cups (300 mL) coconut milk

3 pandan leaves (or pandan extract if you can't find fresh or frozen leaves)

1¼ cups (300 mL) sweetened condensed milk

5 free-run eggs

⅓ cup (80 mL) butter, cut into several small chunks

01. Add the coconut milk and pandan leaves to a blender or food processor and blend until puréed.

02. Pour the coconut-pandan mixture through a cheesecloth-lined sieve or colander set over a bowl. Press down on the mash with the back of a spoon to extract all the milk and flavour; you should end up with about 1 cup (250 mL) of liquid.

03. Add the condensed milk to the coconut-pandan milk and whisk to blend. Once

Chef Li serves Thai doughnuts for dipping into coconut egg jam.

thoroughly blended, transfer the mixture to a lidded heat-proof container. The container must be big enough to hold this milk mixture and the eggs that you'll add later.

04. Prepare a steamer by placing a wire rack or bamboo steamer into a large lidded pot or wok set over high heat—see the sidebar on page 146 for more steaming tips. Add enough water to the pot to just come up to the wire rack or steamer.

05. Bring the water to a rolling boil. Place the lidded container of the coconut-milk mixture on the rack, place the lid on the pot or wok and steam for about 1 hour. Make sure to keep refilling the water so it doesn't boil dry.

06. After 1 hour, remove the container from the steamer and set aside while you beat the eggs with a whisk. When eggs are well beaten, slowly add them to the container of cooked coconut milk, whisking continuously to ensure the eggs don't cook and scramble.

07. Replace the lid on the container, place back on the steamer, and steam for 30 minutes, stirring occasionally to ensure the eggs remain well blended and evenly mixed into the coconut-milk mixture.

08. After 30 minutes, remove the container from steamer, add the butter and stir in until thoroughly incorporated; set aside to cool.

09. Serve cool with pancakes, French toast, fresh tropical fruit salad, doughnuts, over ice cream or in a tropical trifle.

winter

THE WINTER CHICKEN AND GARDEN

THE EGG: WINTER RECIPES

the winter chicken and garden

This may well be the quietest time in the garden, but it's a busy time in the coop and one of the loveliest times in the kitchen. Winter is when I bake, and Christmas is my excuse to make shortbread for celebrations and, naturally, shortbread for breakfast. After all, it's just flour, sugar and butter—and how is that any different from toast with butter and jam? Am I right?

HENHOUSE BEAUTIFUL

Keeping hens in the city or suburbs has many unique challenges, not the least of which may be your human neighbours. If you're keeping a flock on 27 acres in the middle of nowhere, go ahead and house them in Aunt Bessie's old school bus, who's to see? But if your nearest neighbour is three feet away on one side and across a driveway on the other, it's important to make the coop a pretty and seamless addition to the overall house and garden:

- Buy or build the nicest, most fitting coop you can afford; if you live on a street of Victorian row houses, slap some gingerbread on the coop. Try to echo your own house by repeating window box plantings and colour schemes. Can your house's existing shed or garage be retrofitted into a coop?
- Paint the coop to blend in with its surroundings: your house, the garden, your neighbour's house.
- Put in plantings that will help conceal the coop winter, spring, summer and fall—think evergreens, quick-growing vines, something pretty growing up a trellis (maybe grapes or roses) or hydrangea if it's in the shade. Mine is covered in wild grapevines, a somewhat rampant volunteer bittersweet, Virginia creeper and a real show-off clematis. I put in a crabapple at one end, ostrich ferns underneath that and a covered run with a 6-foot (1.8-m) fence and gate. It's pretty well integrated into my property and is in no way an eyesore. Don't give the street anything to complain about.

COOP COUTURE

If you're handy or have a handyperson of your very own, here are a few coops you can draw inspiration from (page 165). Or you can simply buy one. These range from affordable-for-most to wildly extravagant.

CHICKEN FEED AT ITS FINEST

Life is cozy inside the kitchen, but for wintering hens, baby, it's cold outside! They're going to need more high-carb grains and corn in their feed. Seeds and nuts are a real treat—my ladies love

TOP LEFT: From UK-based Omlet, this is the Eglu Go UP. It's made from recycled plastic and welded steel mesh and comes in super stylish colours. Eglu models start at a modest price point and go *up* from there (photo courtesy Omlet).

BOTTOM LEFT: From Creative Coops, the Cute Coop has an iconic look in barn-red and adorable little hen cut outs (photo courtesy Wayfair).

TOP RIGHT: This haut henhouse is a sensational DIY by Karen Bertelsen of *The Art of Doing Stuff*. It took her about two months to build while her hens waited in the shed. As for cost, she admits, "I stopped counting at $1,000" (photo courtesy Karen Bertelsen).

BOTTOM RIGHT: The BReeD RETReaT bears a price tag not for the faint of heart. Designed by Frederik Roijé, it's built in the Netherlands from durable wood and finished in a weather-durable coating (photo courtesy dutchphotography).

peanuts—and suspending a birdseed and suet cake in a basket feeder provides them with a fun activity and fatty supplement. I like to hang it just a little too high for them, so they have to reach and stretch a bit to enjoy it; keeps them warm and fit! On those −20 nights, I'll make the ladies a bowl of hot oatmeal or soft polenta right before bedtime. A crop full of warm starchy goodness is just the thing for a cozy night's sleep. Their feathery coats are snug, but on bitterly cold days, they will be burning calories just trying not to turn into chicksicles!

At the farm store, you'll find two types of adult chicken feed: layer's mash and scratch. Baby chicks have their own feed. The mash is a complete-meal type of feed with calcium and grit added. It's the stuff the poor factory birds live on and supposedly it is nutritionally complete. I imagine it would be like you or me living on some kind of nutrient bar or shake—we'd survive but where's the joy? There's organic or conventional and pellets or crumb to choose from and, as boring as it seems, it really should make up the lion's

share of what the gals eat. In wintertime, I'll make a sort of porridge out of a scoop or two of pellets with a little hot water added; the ladies love it!

Scratch is full of grains and corn, and high in sugars and calories. In winter, it's important to give the girls scratch; they need extra energy just to stay warm. In the summer, when they're foraging like mad, there's enough free-range food available, though they sure do enjoy some scratch as a treat. And remember, never toss it anywhere you don't want the ladies to, well, scratch. Also, keep in mind that any uneaten scratch grain will either sprout or attract varmints.

VEGETARIAN HENS . . . NOT!

My hero, farmer and author Joel Salatin of Polyface Farm in Virginia, recounts a story in his brilliant book *Folks, This Ain't Normal* that speaks to the carnivorous tendencies of hens. As a boy growing up on a farm, one of his first responsibilities was to go out into the woods in winter to hunt small game—squirrels and such—to feed to the chickens. That's right—chickens are meat-eaters, and they need animal protein, especially in the cold season when there are no bugs around.

The spin doctors of factory farming have convinced the average consumer that a vegetarian hen is a healthier, more natural hen, and that her eggs are better for us. Total hooey. A vegetarian hen is a hungry hen that produces washed-out eggs. To be healthy and lay rich, nutritious, flavourful eggs, hens need a varied and balanced diet of greens, animal and bug protein, and grains.

In the warm months, the ladies and I like to play the "turn over the log/brick/stone and hunt for bugs" game. I troll the garden looking for buggy hiding places, the ladies excitedly following along; actually, Miss Vicky usually anticipates where I'm headed and beats me to it, scratching at the next log she'd like turned over, thank you very much!

In one of our expeditions, I turned over one of our favourite stumps—rotting and usually full of potato bugs and millipedes—when a mouse darted out from under. Ginger saw it first, and it was the fastest I'd ever seen her move: she pounced on the mouse like a tiny T. Rex. I was stunned, and kind of impressed. The squeaking was a tad upsetting as she thrashed the life out of the wee beastie, then down the hatch—almost. There was my beautiful red Ginger, running, all drumsticks and bum-fluff, her flock mates in hot pursuit—everyone wanted a piece of that mouse—with its rear end and tail hanging out of her gaping maw. Around and around the garden they went, like hen roller derby, shoulder-checking Ginger in an attempt to steal her quarry. She exploded into a sprint, gaining one precious moment without harassment, and in a flash it was gone. Swallowed whole. Upcycled into the richest egg I enjoyed that summer.

So if you're up for live-trapping and gifting any mice you might have in your house, your ladies will love you for it; just make sure you've not put any mouse poison down. If that's not quite your thing, visit your local exotic pet shop for live mealworms and crickets as wintertime treats. Your ladies will go nuts, and crickets offer them a chance to hunt and have a little fun. Watching hens chase after crickets, especially through the snow, is physical comedy at its best. Failing that, please offer your hens some meat treats through the winter. I give my girls cooked leftovers of anything and everything. Even premium-quality high-protein cat kibble is a good once-in-a-while treat.

Of course, the other component missing in winter is fresh greens. You may have year-round salad in your garden if you live in a warmer zone—keep the best of the bunch for your own dinner and give the ragged leaves to your girls. Or, if your garden is dormant and under snow, you can grow sprouts, wheatgrass or other microgreens in a window or under lights, or purchase

cold frame for the coop

You know what they say: one man's trash is another man's treasure. My eyes are always peeled for discarded windows—there's so much you can do with them. The sunroom attached to my kitchen is the result of a collection of wooden mix-and-match windows from a friend who had the windows in his home upgraded. They also make attractive cold-frame covers for raised beds. I have several raised beds patched together from scrap wood; they're solid enough to attach posts to for resting window frames on. Hoop houses might be more practical—snow slides off the curved roof—but I like the quaint look of glass and love that it's made from salvage.

Of course, your luck with winter gardening will depend on your hardiness zone, but follow a few rules of thumb, stick to cold-tolerant plants and give it a go. A few plant types that don't mind a little nip from Jack Frost are brassicas, some lettuces, some members of the onion family and roots such as carrots, celeriac and parsnips.

Just as cold frames can be built alongside the south-facing wall of a house or garden shed, so too can they be attached to the sunny side of a henhouse. It's a great way to grow greens for the gals all winter long and, of course, this space can be commandeered in early spring to start seedlings for the veggie patch.

wilted greens from the grocery discount rack. And it's not just important for their health, but for the taste, structure and appearance of the eggs they produce—animal and bug protein adds richness and fat, while fresh greens bump up the omegas and deepen the yellow of the yolk.

WATER IN WINTER

Keeping the ladies hydrated in winter can be a bit of a chore. The smaller the amount of water and the shallower the depth, the faster it will freeze. Some folks use electric water heaters, but I've seen what can happen when electricity, water and straw get together, and it's not good. I prefer to give them warm water a few times a day until bedtime. Adding electrolyte powder (essentially sugar and salt) to the water may slow down the freezing a bit; they will appreciate it, as sugar is a food energy that helps them keep warm.

Some folks suggest adding a drop of apple-cider vinegar to winter water to slow its freezing, or in the summer to curtail bacterial growth. Unfortunately, my ladies did not care for the taste, but it's worth trying to see if your flock finds it more agreeable.

EXTENDING DAYLIGHT HOURS

The farther north we go, the longer the summer days are—great for vitamin D and egg laying. But wherever winter gets dark, a light therapy lamp is a great investment for steady egg production year-round. A light therapy lamp is designed to supplement natural sunlight during the winter months and is prescribed to treat Seasonal Affective Disorder in people. From October through April, I use one in the coop for a few hours a day. I'm not trying to turn their home into an egg factory, but do think they appreciate the extra light as much as I do when I bask in the glow of my own light therapy lamp.

On the other hand, allowing hens to live by the rhythms of nature means they get the rest they need to start laying again in the spring. It's a personal choice, and as long as you supplement their diet with meaty protein—mealworms, crickets, meat, eggs, yogurt—and some leafy greens and sprouts, they're fine without extra light.

During really cold snaps, make sure to gather eggs promptly after being laid—if they freeze they expand and bust the shell.

 got the winter blues?

I don't think I've met a gardener who doesn't get a little down in winter. Beyond the lack of Vitamin Sunshine, it's that loss of connection to the soil that depletes us. For me, it's truly like someone I love is leaving me for a long time. When I get back out there—digging, raking, planting and mucking out the coop—I feel like me again . . . the whole me. And this sensation is not just in my imagination: the folks in the lab coats have found evidence suggesting that antidepressant bacteria live in the soil. When we get our hands dirty, some of it invariably gets into our bloodstream via inhalation or perhaps even right though our skin. As the theory goes, the bacterium *Mycobacterium vaccae* makes our brains pump out a bit more serotonin, which makes us more relaxed and happier. Father always said to me that "you gotta eat a peck of dirt before you die." He was on to something—and he was never happier than when he was in his garden or greenhouse.

SIGNE LANGFORD PHOTO

JACK FROST NIPPING AT YOUR . . . COMB?

It's surprising just how hardy hens are—they don't seem to feel the cold much at all—but still, they do have vulnerabilities. Every farmer or seasoned chicken-keeper I've met tells me the same thing: while hens can take the cold, they can't take a draft. And the most pragmatic will say there is no need to heat the coop; in fact, heating a closed coop inhabited by well-hydrated hens can cause it to become too moist and may encourage fungus or mould. That may well be, but I'm a bit of a sucker and spoil my ladies: I want them to be toasty, so I have installed a heater in their

I started with an existing garden shed, added bits and pieces of scrap wood, gave it a lick of whitewash—and Cluckingham Palace was ready for my divas.

well-ventilated coop. If you're not a softie like me, and are not living in the High North, you really don't need one, though most hen-keepers I know have a heat lamp on standby for the most bitter of nights. More on heat lamps in a moment; I'm not a supporter.

Whether you add heat or not, you need to winterize the coop. A friend of mine with a couple of hens has a tiny coop that she simply wraps up with bubble plastic, and her girls do just fine. When my ladies were in my first coop—a 3- × 5-foot (0.9- × 1.5-m) A-frame—I would add thick vapour-barrier plastic to it in the winter. Even now that they're in Cluckingham Palace—an absolutely, um, palatial 100 square feet (9 square metres)!—where they've got a heater, I still make sure there are no drafts by hanging a set of winter curtains inside the door and filling gaps with spray foam.

HEATING THINGS UP

heat lamps: I'm not a fan of heat lamps, and here's why: I've heard too many times how one well-placed jab from the beak of a curious hen, or a drop of cold water flicked up from the drinking station, can cause the bulb to explode, showering the straw below with hot wire filaments and glass. A bulb could also be brought down from its hook in the middle of the night, should the gals get spooked and flap around in the dark. If that happens, a coop can ignite and become a pile of ashes in a matter of minutes; certainly before you've had a chance to grab a bucket of water or a fire extinguisher. Speaking of: I keep an extinguisher hanging by the back door, just inside my kitchen and on the way to the coop, where it's easy to grab in an emergency. Plus, I have set up a smoke alarm in the coop, just in case, and leave a hose ready to go mere feet from it. If you do use

THE WINTER CHICKEN AND GARDEN   169

a heat lamp in the coop (or even a regular light), don't be tempted by bulbs with a shatter-proof protective coating—fumes from the Teflon coating are toxic to birds in enclosed spaces.

ceramic space heaters: While ceramic heaters are pretty safe, they do get quite hot and the hot elements can be exposed from certain angles, potentially igniting dry straw. If you use one, make sure it's secure inside a fireproof container. I placed one inside a large galvanized steel tub on the floor to warm my coop during one winter.

oil space heaters: This is my favourite option. An oil space heater doesn't suck up a river of electricity and doesn't become overly warm to the touch—my adopted mystery-breed, Baby, quite likes sitting right on top of ours for a toasty tummy—and there's nothing aglow to spark a fire.

hot rocks or bricks: This is the most basic of all methods to see your ladies through the coldest of nights: simply heat up a few big rocks or bricks—I fill a large cast iron Dutch oven with lava rocks and heat them up in my oven—wrap them in towels and tuck them into the coop. I used this method when a heater broke down one chilly night, and the ladies huddled around the rocks for warmth and seemed fine.

FOUL-WEATHER FOWL

Keeping a flock in Thunder Bay, Ontario, or other chilly spots where winter temperatures frequently dip down, can present very different challenges from keeping hens in hot, humid southern Florida. Customizing your flock for your climate is a key consideration for backyard hen-keepers and gardeners—one size does not fit all.

In the chilly north, a lush comb is a liability—one deep freeze and it will succumb to frostbite. A handsome bird with a showy comb will do much better in the southern United States or other hot spots where that flap of blood-rich flesh will act as a heat disperser, much like the floppy ears of an elephant do.

Of course, the size of the breed matters too. While I don't worry about my fat, fluffy ladies in the cold, I used to fret terribly about little Nugget—my darling deceased Sebright bantam. She looked so miserable on the coldest days that I would bring her inside to warm up for a bit.

I asked Lisa Steele of the *Fresh Eggs Daily* blog, who keeps hens on her Virginia farm, about her favourite breeds: "We get both hot and humid in the summer, with temperatures near 100F [38C], and also cold, down into the single digits in the winter. For me, heat-tolerant breeds are a bit more important, since most chickens are naturally cold-hardy." Here are Lisa's picks for chicks that can take the heat *and* stand the cold!

ameraucana: Black or blue hens that lay pretty blue eggs. Besides their gorgeous eggs, these hens are both cold-hardy and heat-tolerant.

---

there's one in every flock: the night owl

Hens are wonderful about heading back to the run or coop as the sun starts to set. Right on cue, and in an orderly procession—usually single file—the ladies will head home to safety. Lights out is a different matter. Most of my girls are early to bed and early to rise, but there's always one who figures if the human is up, then she should be too. I drop by the coop once they should be settled to hit the light switch and Madame Night Owl pops off her perch to see what's for midnight snacks. (Note to self: install light switch on the outside of the coop.)

Sweet Nugget has her "blanket," or tummy feathers, spread over her toes against the cold. It's something that all birds do, from budgies to eagles!

blue andalusian: Greyish-blue hens with large combs that lay white eggs. The large combs help keep them cool in summer.

lavender orpington: The paler-coloured "sisters" of the Black Australorp. Blue-coloured hens that lay pale-tan eggs. Very docile, light coloured and tend to be heat-tolerant.

mottled java: Pretty speckled black and white hens that lay pale-tan eggs. Both cold-hardy and heat-tolerant.

penedesenca: Sleek hens that lay chocolate-brown eggs and are extremely heat-tolerant.

Lisa also has some helpful cold-weather tips:

- First, all hen-keepers agree that in cold climates breeds with small or flat combs—such as rose or pea combs—are best. "Easter Egger, Buckeye, Ameraucana and Wyandotte fare far better in the cold than breeds with larger combs such as Andalusian and Leghorn. Obviously, roosters with large combs and wattles will be the most vulnerable."

- And she suggests applying a coating to the vulnerable bits as a preventative. "Try coating large combs and wattles with softened coconut oil or Waxelene, an all-natural alternative to petroleum jelly."

KEEPING A COZY COOP

Mara Bacsujlaky lives in Fairbanks, Alaska, awfully far north for the descendants of a flashy jungle bird, and tells me her flock gets by just fine, thank you very much! "For cold climates, chicken breeds with rose combs, or very small combs close to the head, are preferred." But there's more to keeping a flock of laying hens healthy and laying through an Alaskan winter, says Mara, who shares some tips:

- Build a coop small enough to conserve heat but with enough room for the ladies to roam,

cold climate cluck

The Chantecler is the only true Canadian breed, and was developed to tolerate cold winters. A sturdy bird, it's less susceptible to frostbite with tiny combs and wattles that lie close to the body for warmth.

Mara Bacsujlaky's hens still enjoy a dirt bath, even in the depths of an Alaskan winter!

since there are going to be long stretches of time—potentially four to five months—when it'll be too cold to go outside.

- Insulate the walls and roof of the coop.
- Maintain the number of birds for which the henhouse is sized; if your coop can accommodate 12 hens, keeping only 6 means you'll need to supply extra heat. Hens snuggle up together for warmth and each produces a fair bit of body heat, so the more the merrier . . . and toastier. And by toasty, I mean above freezing.
- Hens also blow off a fair bit of steam, well, moisture actually, and dampness can be a problem, allowing mould to grow and frostbite to develop on combs and even toes. A little dry heat and a small fan to circulate the air will take care of that, and even though it's cold

outside (and in), ventilation is important; you don't need or want an airtight coop, otherwise ammonia—a by-product of their droppings—can build up and that's very unhealthy for them. Just like all birds, chickens have highly responsive and sensitive respiratory systems.

- Give the girls two types of perches on which to roost: a pole they can wrap their feet around to perch, and a flat surface they can squat down on, which keeps their feet extra cozy.
- Mara's birds usually go outside when the mercury hits 25F (–4C) or warmer, even if there is deep snow on the ground; it's important to provide a covered run where the birds can still peck, scratch and dust bathe, even in the dead of winter.
- Try the deep-litter method: that's when you cover the floor of the coop with plenty of straw—about 6 to 12 inches (15 to 30 cm)—and just sort of "fluff" it or move it around a bit every day. That lets the dry or frozen droppings—poopsicles, in polite company—sift to the bottom. It's what Mara does, and it's what I do, and I swear by it. It's cold, so the straw doesn't get stinky, and it really helps to keep the coop warm. This is what I'll muck out in the spring, much to the delight of my garden, the sparrows and the ladies too, since they get to scratch through it all looking for lost bits of corn. Mara is more vigilant than I am, but then I only have a few ladies and they are never cooped up for more than a couple of days at a stretch. She'll muck out the coop, or at least half of it, every two weeks or so, or sometimes she'll just add more straw.
- Another challenge of keeping laying hens at northern latitudes—especially as far north as Alaska—is the amount of daylight. Mara tells me, "In Fairbanks at the peak of winter

we have four hours of very low, dim daylight. This is not enough natural light to keep hens laying through a winter; between 12 and 14 hours of artificial light is required, so I start putting my hens on a timed light in mid-September. Northern hens need artificial light from September to March."

RECYCLING CHRISTMAS TREES INTO THE COOP AND GARDEN

Drag home a discarded Christmas tree or two, or as many as your garden can use—they're very useful in the garden and coop. I just prop them up in the coop until I get around to dealing with them; the birds are happy for the extra shelter. When I have the time, I cut off all the branches and add some to my compost, lay some around the garden beds as weed-suppressing hen deterrents, and give some to the ladies for their coop and run. The piney scent is lovely and bugs don't care for it. In the shaded part of my garden, next to the coop, I'm building up my Ontario woodland garden, so that's where trunks end up, to act as a fallen trees or "mother logs" would do in the forest.

Don't bring home a tree all tangled up with tinsel or covered in that spray-on snow, though.

The ladies' luxurious digs, Cluckingham Palace, in winter. In the early evening, when the light is on inside, the glow in the window is such a cozy sight.

And keep in mind some trees are treated with fire-retardant chemicals. Try to determine if it's from a clean source before you introduce a tree to the henhouse, or allow it to sit out in the elements for a few months first.

the egg: winter recipes

Cooking, shopping and eating with the seasons can seem to some folks an unnecessary exercise in deprivation. But that's the wrong way to look at it. Once you make the mental shift to eating in sync with the seasons, you no longer want asparagus in November or blueberries in January; not when you've had your fill—and then some—of what your area's farmers produce in season.

SIGNE LANGFORD PHOTO

To be honest, eating seasonally in the North can be challenging and one can grow weary of all those tubers, roots and squash. Traditionally, summer's bounty would have been put up in jars and available all winter long; today we just pop out to the grocery store for a tin of peaches or even—and I *really* don't recommend it—a basket of those flavourless hard-as-rocks-and-white-inside strawberries.

But, consider winter's celebratory feasts—the foods are seasonal, delicious and a shining example of what eating in the off-season can be. Look for what you can find locally wherever you are, and don't forget that there's always a heart-warming meal—or luscious glass of homemade Canadiana Eggnog—to be had right from your very own backyard, courtesy of your happy hens.

174

eggs in dents and holes: delicious!

Making depressions and holes in other foods to turn them into cooking vessels for eggs is a time-honoured culinary tradition. A slice of bread is the simplest. It's tasty, creative and makes a fun and easy first foray into the kitchen for kids. Muffin tins are also great for cooking up eggs in edible cups. If you can grease it, fit it into a muffin tin and make room for an egg, you can use it: a slice of bread, ham, strips of bacon, shredded potato, corn tortilla, and on and on . . .

To get the whole experience right, use these tips and check out the inspiration below:

- Don't hold back on the fat—butter, olive oil and bacon fat are good, flavourful choices that will give you crispy fried bread, or whatever else you use.
- The egg can be whole or scrambled.
- When cooking an egg in a bready thing, always fry the cut-out bit of bread too, and serve it alongside for dipping. And fry the first side until golden before adding the egg and flipping.

eight ways to try

THE CLASSIC: Fry slices of bread with holes cookie-cuttered out of the centres and an egg plopped into each. To make both sides of the bread really crispy without ending up with a hard yolk, fry the first side without the egg, flip, drop in the egg and cook until set, then flip back over for a few seconds more.

VEGGIE RING: A big, fat onion ring, a ring of sweet bell pepper or even a thinly sliced, hollowed-out ring of squash will work. Use a smaller egg or it may well runneth over.

GILDING THE LILY: Assemble a classic grilled cheese sandwich and cookie-cutter out the middle before frying it. Melt fat of choice in a skillet and grill both the sandwich edges and the centre, flip, then add an egg to the hole.

EXTREME GILDED LILY: The above, but with the addition of a slice of peameal bacon or ham.

BIGGER THAN TEXAS TOAST: Start with a loaf of uncut bread—your favourite kind—then slice off a 3-inch (7.5-cm) thick piece, cut out a hole, and fry just as The Classic.

SWEETIE PIE: Start with challah or sweet egg bread, cut out a hole, add a scrambled egg and fry in butter. Serve with maple syrup or dust with icing sugar.

BET: That's bacon, egg and tomato. Cut a firm medium-sized tomato in half, hollow out, add an egg into each half and top with finely chopped raw bacon. Bake at 400F (205C) until the bacon is crispy and the egg is set.

DO THE MASH: Butter an oven-safe dish, spread in leftover mashed potatoes (warmed first in the microwave so they are easy to work with) and make a dent deep enough to hold an egg. Add an egg—whole or scrambled—to the dent, sprinkle with grated cheese and bake at 400F (205C) until cheese is melted and egg is set.

eggnog french toast

SERVES 2

● ●

I can't think of a more perfect Christmas morning breakfast than this. It's easy, quick and flexible—use whatever bread you like or happen to have on hand. I love cinnamon raisin bread for this.

2 free-run eggs
⅔ cup (160 mL) Canadiana Eggnog, recipe
   on page 186 (or use organic store-bought)
2–3 Tbsp (30–45 mL) butter for the pan,
   more as needed
6 slices of bread, each about 1 inch (2.5 cm) thick

01. In a wide bowl, whisk the eggs and eggnog until very well blended.

02. Heat your largest skillet or griddle over medium heat. Add about 2 teaspoons (10 mL) of butter for each batch of bread you fry. Add more as needed if it gets absorbed by the bread too quickly.

03. Dip the bread slices into the egg mixture, 2 at a time, and press down to submerge and soak. Pull the slices out, let the excess drip off and add to skillet. Fry on each side for about 5 minutes or until golden. The bread will puff up a bit.

04. Transfer to a tray in a warm oven while you fry up the rest of the slices.

05. Serve with maple syrup or Maple-Cranberry Sauce or both! What the hey, it's Christmas!

French toast is a real swinger, going from sweet to savoury without a moment's hesitation! How about some savoury French toast for lunch? Start with a traditional egg and milk dunking mixture, but instead of vanilla, add salt and pepper, spices or herbs. And for the bread, start with a more savoury loaf: olive boule, sun-dried tomato focaccia, onion buns or cheese bread. Fry in olive oil or butter, and instead of topping with maple syrup or fruit, top with a savoury mushroom gravy, bacon and caramelized onion jam, warm tomato sauce or cheese sauce.

maple-cranberry sauce

MAKES ABOUT 1 CUP (250 ML)

● ●

½ cup (120 mL) frozen or fresh cranberries
¼ cup (60 mL) freshly squeezed orange juice
   (about half a large orange)
¼ cup (60 mL) maple syrup
2 Tbsp (30 mL) brandy, rye or dark rum (optional)

01. Add all ingredients to a small saucepan over medium-high heat. Bring up to a very gentle boil, just slightly more than a simmer. Stir occasionally.

02. After about 5 minutes the cranberries should be split and soft; smoosh them with your spoon to break them down further. For a grownup breakfast, stir in brandy, rye or dark rum. Transfer to jar or other serving vessel and enjoy warm or cold.

sun and cloud eggs

SERVES 4

Well, that's what I'm calling it, because I'm not sure they have an agreed upon official name, and while this isn't a hearty dish or even the most wowing flavour-wise, I think it's something we should all make at least once, just because it's kind of neat and I think kids would get a real kick out of it. The sun is the yolk and the cloud is the fluffy egg white it sits on.

4 Tbsp (60 mL) butter, divided
4 free-run eggs
Fine sea salt to taste
Freshly ground black pepper to taste
1–2 Tbsp (15–30 mL) finely chopped fresh
    flat-leaf parsley, chives or your favourite herb
    for garnish

01. Preheat oven to 450F (230C).

02. Melt 2 tablespoons (30 mL) butter in a cast iron or other oven-safe skillet; about a 10-inch (25-cm) pan will do. Remove from heat and let cool.

03. Meanwhile, separate the eggs. I find it easiest to set up four wee dishes or cups to place each yolk into. That will make it super easy to place the yolks onto the "clouds" later.

04. Add the whites into a bowl that you've wiped out with a bit of lemon juice or vinegar. With electric beaters or in the bowl of a stand mixer with the whisk attachment, beat the whites until fluffy stiff peaks form.

05. When the pan is cool enough, grease the sides with 1 tablespoon (15 mL) butter. With a large spoon, make 4 "clouds" of whites in the skillet. Using the back of the spoon, make a depression in each.

06. Deposit a yolk into each dented cloud, and season the yolks with salt and pepper and the remaining butter.

07. Set skillet over medium heat. Fry until the bottoms of the whites begin to turn golden.

08. Pop into the oven and bake for 7 minutes or so, or until yolks are set but not solid and the butter has melted.

09. Garnish with a sprinkling of finely chopped fresh herbs—whatever you like best.

cheesy variation: Sprinkle about ¼ cup (60 mL) **of your favourite grated cheese** over the yolks just before popping into the oven.

finnish egg butter

MAKES ABOUT 3 CUPS (710 ML)

Richer than rich, this is a dish not for the faint or fluttery of heart. Might I suggest a day of log splitting in sub-zero temperatures to work up an appetite?

8 free-run eggs
½ cup + 1 Tbsp (135 mL) cold butter
1 Tbsp (15 mL) finely chopped fresh chives
Sea salt and freshly ground pepper to taste

01. Allow eggs to come to room temperature. Add eggs to a pot of cold water to cover, place over medium heat and bring to a gentle boil. Boil for about 5 minutes, remove from heat and set aside to cool for about 20 minutes; leave the eggs in the pot of water.
02. When cool enough to handle, but still a little warm, peel and add eggs to a large bowl with the butter. Using a large fork, mash the butter and eggs together well to combine.
03. Stir in the chives, salt and pepper. Taste and adjust salt and pepper if needed.
04. Serve with bread or crackers for slathering.

persian eggs

SERVES 6

This is the king of egg-in-dent dishes, no contest!

2 Tbsp (30 mL) extra-virgin olive oil

1 Tbsp (15 mL) butter

1 cup (250 mL) sliced halloumi or Canadian
   Guernsey Girl (about 9 oz/250 g)

1 small purple onion, finely chopped

3 cloves garlic, finely chopped

3 small red, yellow and orange bell peppers,
   julienned

2 Tbsp (30 mL) za'atar

¼ tsp (1 mL) sea salt or more to taste

Freshly ground pepper to taste

2½ cups (600 mL) coarsely chopped ripe red,
   yellow and orange tomatoes (about 5 small)

1 Tbsp (15 mL) finely chopped flat-leaf parsley

3 Tbsp (45 mL) honey

14 oz (398 mL) can artichoke hearts,
   halved and very well drained

6 free-run eggs

01. Preheat oven to 400F (205C).

02. Into a large oven-safe skillet over medium-high heat (I love cast iron or copper for this), add the oil, butter and halloumi; fry until lightly golden on first side, about 3 minutes. Flip and fry until golden on the second side, about 3 minutes. Transfer from skillet to plate and set aside.

03. Add the onion, garlic and peppers; stir and cook over medium heat until they soften and turn colour, about 5 minutes. Add the za'atar, salt and pepper and cook, stirring, for about 2 minutes more.

04. Add the tomatoes, parsley and honey; stir and cook until the tomatoes start to break down a bit, about 5 minutes. Add the artichoke hearts, stir, then remove from heat.

05. With the back of a spoon, make 6 deep depressions in the mixture, crack an egg into each and place pieces of halloumi between the eggs and in any empty spots. If there is leftover halloumi, then it's the cook's treat!

06. Pop into the oven and bake for 20 to 25 minutes, or until eggs are just set.

07. Bring some harissa—a Middle Eastern hot sauce—to the table, and serve with warm pita bread, sliced cucumbers and *labneh*, an extra-thick, tangy full-fat yogurt.

winter spanish tortilla

SERVES 6

Don't confuse a Spanish tortilla with a Mexican tortilla. The latter is the familiar flatbread we wrap tasty stuff up with, whereas a Spanish tortilla is more akin to a frittata, only better—at least, I think so. I find Spanish tortillas are at their best about 40 minutes to an hour after coming out of the oven, when they're at room temperature—not hot, but not cold either. Complete this lunch or light dinner with a side of greens from the garden dressed with sherry vinaigrette.

1 medium Yukon Gold potato, scrubbed

1 small sweet potato, peeled

10 free-run eggs

¼ tsp (1 mL) sea salt, or more to taste

¼ tsp (1 mL) black pepper, or more to taste

¼ cup (60 mL) finely chopped Italian
    (flat-leaf) parsley ¼ cup (60 mL) olive oil

1 medium red onion, finely diced

Half a red pepper, finely diced

½ cup (120 mL) thin coins of chorizo, mild or hot

3 cloves garlic, minced

½ tsp (2.5 mL) smoked Spanish paprika

⅓ cup (80 mL) pitted Spanish olives (or substitute
    Kalamata olives packed in oil)

¼ cup (60 mL) grated Manchego or pecorino
    cheese for garnish, or to taste

01. Preheat oven to 350F (180C).

02. Slice the 2 potatoes very thin using a mandolin or a very sharp chef's knife or, what I prefer, the single blade side of a box grater. I find that's the perfect thickness and it's not a bother to set up like a mandolin, while still being speedy to do.

03. In a medium bowl, whisk the eggs, sea salt and pepper and finely chopped parsley. Set aside.

04. In a large (about 10-inch/25-cm) cast iron skillet (or other oven-safe skillet) over medium heat, add the olive oil, onion, red pepper, chorizo, garlic and paprika and fry, stirring often, for about 5 minutes, or until the onions are beginning to colour.

05. Add the potatoes and olives; stir to blend and fry for a further 5 minutes.

06. Give the eggs one more whisking and pour into the pan, pouring slowly over the other ingredients. Give the pan a few good jiggles and shakes to let the egg mixture settle down to the bottom and into all the nooks and crannies.

07. Transfer to oven and bake for about 15 to 20 minutes, or until the tortilla is puffed somewhat and beginning to turn a very light golden on top. Allow to cool for at least 20 minutes before serving; trust me, the flavours just sing when warmish. Too hot and they're muted.

08. To serve, offer the grated cheese or, better yet, bring the block of cheese to the table with a Microplane and let folks help themselves.

SIGNE LANGFORD PHOTO

An layer of ice clings to the bare winter vines that creep across some hen folk art I made for the run.

vegetarian variation: Simply omit the chorizo or replace it with coins of **veggie hot dog.** You'll need to add **1 teaspoon (5 mL) oil and 1 teaspoon (5 mL) paprika** to the pan with the veggie dog coins to make up for the fat and flavour that would have been contributed by the chorizo. Fry the veggie dog coins until crispy brown.

peels-schmeels

I don't peel potatoes unless the Queen is coming to dinner. There is good stuff in those peels, and the ladies don't eat them, so I may as well, right? Just scrub the heck out of them, pick off any eyes and, of course, trim off any blemishes or green bits. The green parts are toxic.

redemption egg foo young

SERVES 2

I failed Home Ec. I disappointed Teacher with my Chinese dinner; I still don't know where I went wrong. Making a Chinese meal from scratch in small-town Quebec in the 1970s was a tall order. Mother only had a few cookbooks to work from, so I went with a menu of recipes found in the *Five Roses Cook Book* and the *LIFE Picture Cook Book* from 1958. I'm going for redemption with this brilliant egg foo young.

4 Tbsp (60 mL) vegetable oil, divided
1 shallot, minced
2 cloves garlic, minced
Half a green pepper, finely diced
1 celery stalk, finely diced
2 scallions, finely sliced, divided
1 cup (250 mL) fresh bean sprouts, washed and dried
10 wild-caught shrimp or BC spot prawns, peeled and deveined
4 free-run eggs

SAUCE

¾ cup (180 mL) organic chicken stock
1 Tbsp (15 mL) good-quality soy sauce
1 Tbsp (15 mL) oyster sauce
1 Tbsp (15 mL) seasoned rice vinegar
1 Tbsp (15 mL) mirin or Chinese rice wine
1 tsp (5 mL) coconut sugar (or substitute granulated sugar)
2 tsp (10 mL) cornstarch

01. Add about 2 tablespoons (30 mL) oil to a medium skillet over high heat.

02. Add shallot, garlic, green pepper, celery and most of the scallions, reserving some scallions for garnish; fry, stirring constantly, for about 1 to 2 minutes or until just softened.

03. Add the well-drained bean sprouts; fry, stirring constantly, for another minute.

04. Add the shrimp; fry until just turning pink and opaque. Transfer shrimp and sprout mixture to a dish and set aside. Put the pan to one side and allow it to cool.

05. While the pan is cooling, prepare the sauce. In a medium bowl, whisk together all sauce ingredients until well blended, with no cornstarch lumps. Set aside.

06. In a large bowl using a fork, whisk the eggs until well beaten. Add the slightly cooled shrimp and sprout mixture to the beaten eggs and stir to combine.

07. Place the skillet back over medium-high heat and add the remaining 2 tablespoons (30 mL) oil.

08. Pour the egg mixture into the skillet and fry for about 2 minutes, or until the edges start turning ever so slightly golden.

09. Either flip and cook the other side or place under a broiler until the top is set. Transfer the egg foo young to a platter, and pour the sauce mixture into the skillet. Turn heat up to high and stir constantly to thicken sauce, about 3 to 5 minutes.

10. Garnish with the remaining chopped scallion, and if you like your dinner to bite back, add a finely minced hot chili. Serve with the sauce on the side, and some sticky rice if you like.

canadiana eggnog

SERVES 8

My father was not a New Age man. He wasn't a fan of "women's lib," as it was known when I was growing up. I made it through my entire childhood without ever seeing him do the groceries. His job was to drive Mother—and sometimes me—to the local IGA or A&P (depending on who had what on sale) and wait in the car with the radio on. Sometimes, out of curiosity, peckishness or because he wanted the latest *Time* magazine, he'd wander inside. He'd drift around the aisles, snacking on a bag of black licorice or jar of roasted peanuts he'd plucked from a shelf. He'd pay for his goodies and head back to his den on wheels before Mother and I were done. He was the kind of man who went shopping at the hardware store, the garden centre and the liquor store. Maybe The Bay if he needed something for his studio—Father was a photographer—but *not* the grocery store.

Until November. That's when the rules of engagement changed—because that's when the first shipment of eggnog landed in the dairy case. He had a sixth sense for it. And it was the sight of him coming home from work, a carton in each hand—one already opened from swigs he took in the car or in the cashier's line—that meant the season of celebration had officially begun. Here is my proud Canadian variation of this Christmas classic.

1 vanilla bean, split lengthwise and scraped
3 cups (710 mL) organic 3.5 percent milk
1 cup (250 mL) organic 35 percent cream
3 cinnamon sticks, about 2 inches (5 cm) long
½ tsp (2.5 mL) freshly grated nutmeg
5 free-run eggs, separated
⅔ cup (160 mL) maple syrup
¾ cup (180 mL) Canadian Club rye
1 Tbsp (15 mL) super-fine (berry) sugar
Whipped cream, for garnish (optional)
Maple sugar or maple flakes, for garnish (optional)

01. Add the vanilla bean and paste to a deep, heavy-bottomed saucepan. Over medium heat, add the milk, cream, cinnamon sticks and nutmeg and whisk to break up the vanilla seeds.

02. Bring to a gentle boil (this should take about 5 to 10 minutes) then remove from heat. Set aside to allow the flavours to infuse the milk and cream for about 10 minutes. Remove and discard the cinnamon sticks and vanilla bean.

03. In a large bowl using a whisk, or in the bowl of a stand mixer, beat the egg yolks with the maple syrup until well combined. Very slowly add in the milk and cream mixture a bit at a time to temper the yolks until completely incorporated. Beat constantly so that the egg yolks don't cook and scramble.

04. Add the rye and blend in.

05. Wipe out a large bowl with a tiny drop of vinegar and a clean rag. Add the egg whites and sugar and with a stand mixer or electric hand beaters, beat the egg whites until peaks form. Add the egg whites to the milk and cream mixture and gently whisk in to combine.

06. Transfer to an airtight container and refrigerate for at least 3 hours, or until well chilled.

07. To serve, pour or ladle into small glasses—this stuff is rich! And this might be a tad indulgent, but sometimes—and if not at Christmas, then when?—top with a dollop of whipped cream and a sprinkling of grated maple sugar or maple flakes, and perhaps a dash more rye should you be feeling particularly spirited!

08. Keep leftovers in the fridge for up to 3 days in an airtight container.

tip

If you're a vanilla fanatic, try adding a vanilla bean to a small bottle or mickey of rye about 2 weeks before making this recipe. The rye that's left over is gorgeous straight up over ice.

vanilla coeur à la crème with blueberry maple compote

MAKES 4 INDIVIDUAL MOULDS OR 1 FAMILY-SIZE HEART AND ABOUT 1¼ CUPS (300 ML) COMPOTE

I'm not sure what came first historically—the mould or the recipe—but I know what came first for me and that was the mould. I saw these pretty little heart-shaped dishes from Quebec craftswoman Edith Bourgault, and I wanted to know what they were for. In the Anjou region of France, where this recipe was created, it's made with a fresh soft farmer's cheese called *fromage blanc*, hard to find outside of Europe or possibly Quebec. In the rest of North America, mascarpone, quark or cream cheese will do. I favour mascarpone because, well, it's mascarpone! Seriously creamy and decadent.

Anyway, since I'm the kind who offers my heart up on a platter, this recipe for romance suits me just fine, any time of year.

1 vanilla bean, split lengthwise and scraped
    (reserve pod)
¾ cup (180 mL) organic 35 percent cream
1 Tbsp (15 mL) icing sugar
4 oz (110 g) mascarpone (about ½ cup/120 mL)
6 oz (170 g) chèvre, at room temperature
    (about 1¼ cups/300 mL)
2 Tbsp (30 mL) lemon juice (about half a lemon)
⅓ cup (80 mL) runny honey
2 free-run egg whites

BLUEBERRY MAPLE COMPOTE

1 cup (250 mL) blueberries (frozen wild berries
    have the best flavour)
¼ cup (60 mL) pure maple syrup
¼ cup (60 mL) ruby port
1 vanilla bean, split lengthwise and scraped

01. Rinse two 12-inch (30-cm) square pieces of cheesecloth in cold water and wring dry. Line 2 heart-shaped *coeur à la crème* moulds with the cheesecloth, letting the cheesecloth drape over the sides of the moulds. Set heart moulds onto a baking pan, tray or plate; set aside.

02. Add vanilla bean paste to a large bowl. Add the cream and icing sugar and whip to soft peaks with an electric beater.

03. In another large bowl with an electric beater, blend the mascarpone with the chèvre, lemon juice and honey until very smooth. Set aside.

04. In a medium bowl—wiped clean with a splash of lemon juice—beat the egg whites until stiff peaks form. Set aside.

05. Now add the whipped cream and whipped egg whites to the large bowl with the cheese mixture and, using a rubber spatula, gently fold until well combined.

continued on page 190

Lizzy Borden staying warm in the freshly whitewashed coop. A single incandescent bulb is sometimes enough to take the sting out of the cold. However, I've since replaced that glamorous lamp with a light therapy lamp.

06. Add the cheese and cream mixture to the prepared moulds, folding the overhanging cheesecloth back over the filled moulds. Place in the fridge to drain and firm up for at least 6 hours; overnight is much better.

07. While the moulds are setting up, make the Blueberry Maple Compote.

08. Into a medium saucepan over medium heat, add the blueberries, maple syrup, port and scraped vanilla bean halves. Bring to a simmer, stirring often; you may need to decrease heat to medium-low. Simmer for about 15 min-utes, or until reduced and thickened, stirring often. Set aside to cool to room temperature. Compote can be made ahead and refrigerated overnight.

09. To serve, peel back the excess cheesecloth, set a plate on top of the mould and invert. Carefully lift off the mould and gently peel away the cheesecloth; inspect for stray cotton threads. Spoon some of the compote on the plate and offer more in a small pitcher or even a gravy boat.

chicken and garden index

SHE HATCHED AN IDEA

recipe index

about the contributors

Signe Langford is a chef, Toronto food writer and backyard chicken fanatic. She is a frequent contributor to the *Globe and Mail, National Post, Toronto Life, Canadian Living* and *Garden Making*.

Donna Griffith is a Toronto-based photographer who shoots food and drink, homes and gardens, people and animals. She doesn't have her own backyard flock—*yet*—but she does enjoy the eggs she mooches from friends who do.

Illustrator **Sophia Saunders** is a Toronto-based artist specializing in hand-made and printed linocuts and ink drawings.

Signe Langford